CANADA

CANADA

PHOTOGRAPHED BY

PETER VARLEY

INTRODUCTION BY KILDARE DOBBS

185 ILLUSTRATIONS

18 IN COLOUR

TORONTO

MACMILLAN OF CANADA

PRINTED IN GREAT BRITAIN BY JARROLD AND SONS LTD, NORWICH

Contents

Notes on the plates by James W. Bacque

*Additional photographs for this book were supplied
by six Toronto photographers:
Ray Webber (Labrador), Horst Ehricht (Yukon),
Herbert Taylor (the High Arctic), George Hunter (Winnipeg),
Freeman Patterson (Toronto), and
John de Visser (New Brunswick, Prince Edward Island, Saskatchewan)*

Introduction

I

Men and nations live by imagination, by the dreams that relate them to their land and its past. It is in these myths that one looks, cautiously, for national character. The myth of the Frontier, for example. There actually was – and there still is – a Frontier in Canada. Prospectors, trappers, and lumberjacks still brawl in the boom-town honky-tonks and beer-parlours. Mounties still occasionally hitch up a dog-team to go out and get their man on the frozen tundra. I have talked to Beaver Indians in their teepees by the Halfway River in northern British Columbia: they actually did wear beaded moccasins and speak like the redskins in television serials. To this extent myth may accord with fact.

Yet the myth may be misleading. The prospector, more scientist than rough-neck, is not what he was: 'The day of the jackass leading the jackass is gone', as one of them told me. And the trapper – the trapper is vanishing, ruined by competition from the fur-farms. The lumberjack has abandoned his axe for a buzz-saw and turns out to be a family man and a church-goer. As for the Mountie, he may well be a youth with pimples, interested in dogs only if their owners have failed to license them. And the Beaver Indians, wearing galoshes over their moccasins, are listening to pop music on transistor radios. Finally, all these people and the Frontier itself are as remote from the experience of most ordinary Canadians as they are from the experience of a bank-clerk in the Bronx or a Stevenage typist. Does this destroy the myth? Not at all.

For in the secret places of his imagination every Canadian sawing firewood at his summer cottage is a lumberjack, every suburbanite on skis a *coureur de bois*, every Sunday canoer a *voyageur*. The myth (as beer advertisers well understand) even influences his drinking. He attacks each beer as if it were his first after months of abstinence in the bush.

The myth of the Frontier is, of course, shared with other North Americans, like the myths of triumphant free enterprise and of the West. There are also more definitive myths which are uniquely Canadian: myths of the United Empire Loyalists, of the conquered but undefeated French Canadians, of the 'true North strong and free'. To call them myths is not to deny their truth. Some of them are rooted in the facts of history and geography.

Canada is the biggest small nation in the world. Surpassed in size only by the U.S.S.R. and China, it covers almost four million square miles of the earth's surface. Of this immense territory a mere half-million square miles is effectively occupied, and 90 per cent of its comparatively small population of twenty-one million is huddled in a narrow band of settlements within three hundred miles of the United States border. Nor is this small nation uniform in language and culture. Approximately 20 per cent of Canadians, mostly in the province of Quebec, speak French only. About 67 per cent speak only English. And though a further 12 per cent (again, mostly in Quebec) speak both languages, approximately 1.3 per cent of Canadians speak neither. Other significant minorities speak German, Italian, Ukrainian, Chinese, Japanese, Hungarian – and in Cape Breton, Nova Scotia, there are some hundreds of descendants of immigrant Scottish Highlanders whose mother-tongue is still Gaelic.

This plural society exists in the shadow of the richest and most powerful nation in the history of the world. Its ten self-governing provinces are ranged in Indian file along the northern border of the United States for a distance of almost 4,000 miles. Nova Scotia, New Brunswick, Quebec, Ontario, Manitoba, Saskatchewan, Alberta, British Columbia: they follow one another, east to west, like so many stops on the transcontinental railway that made Confederation possible. Ferries join Newfoundland, a latecomer to Confederation (1949), and Prince Edward Island to the railway system. Each region is a northward extension of a similar one in the United States: the Maritime or Atlantic provinces are part of the New England Appalachians; Quebec and Ontario are on the lower and upper reaches of the St. Lawrence River system; the Prairie Provinces are part of the great plains; British Columbia, almost entirely mountainous, is a segment of the continent's high rocky spine, the cordillera that runs along the Pacific from Alaska to Mexico.

The railway (or rather two railways, the privately owned Canadian Pacific and the State's Canadian National) is a straight line ruled from ocean to ocean by the chief engineer of Confederation, Canada's first prime minister, Sir John A. Macdonald. 'The railway line, that tenuous thread which bound Canada to both the great oceans and made her a nation, lay with one end in the darkness of Nova Scotia and the other in a British Columbia noon.' The thought occurs with the force of an epiphany to a character in one of the novels of Hugh MacLennan, an eloquent writer on national themes. Perhaps no one but a Canadian could think of a railway in just that way. More – perhaps no one but a Canadian who has deliberately cultivated a national consciousness.

Travelling on the transcontinental passenger trains, one is reminded that the great age of railways that devised Confederation has gone for ever. Most travellers, business men or vacationers in a hurry, prefer to cross Canada by jet airliner. The trains are half empty. Powerful diesel locomotives have displaced steam, but the coaches retain the comfort of an earlier age. White-jacketed Negro porters, the starched linen and gleaming silver of dining-cars, the curiously Victorian uniforms of conductors and other officials, are pleasantly evocative of the nineteenth century. The Canada viewed in a gentlemanly way from dome-cars or the windows of luxurious 'drawing-rooms' (significant archaism) is all Sir John Macdonald's.

This Canada of the railway is only a fraction of the whole country. There is also the older Canada of the waterways. The vast river-system of the St. Lawrence and the Great Lakes carried seventeenth-century explorers, fur-traders, and missionaries of New France deep into the continent. They and their rivals and successors of the fur-trading companies – the Hudson's Bay, XY, and North West companies – were to cast a web of forts and trading-posts over the whole land, a fur empire with headquarters in London and Montreal, its birch-bark canoes and flat-bottomed York boats plying the myriad lakes and rivers of the Canadian Shield.

The Shield is an immense geophysical feature peculiar to Canada.

Its nearly two million square miles of hard Precambrian rock coils round Hudson Bay, crossing the north of all the provinces from Newfoundland to Saskatchewan. In its southern reaches, which cover most of Ontario and Quebec, it is a country of forests, lakes, rivers, and rocky outcrops, a beautiful, implacable wilderness. It is utterly intractable to cultivation.

Harold A. Innis, the great economic historian, long ago stressed the Shield's formative influence: 'Canada emerged as a political entity with boundaries largely determined by the fur trade. These boundaries included a vast north temperate land area extending from the Atlantic to the Pacific and dominated by the Canadian Shield. The present Dominion emerged not in spite of geography but because of it.'

By the turn of the eighteenth and nineteenth centuries the trader-explorers Alexander Mackenzie and Simon Fraser had crossed the continental divide and struggled overland to the Pacific. Some notion of the scale of these activities is hinted in a few statistics of Canada's waterways. The St. Lawrence system is 2,000 miles long. Lake Ontario, smallest of its great lakes, has an area of 7,540 square miles; Lake Superior, the largest (the 'shining big sea water' of Longfellow's *Hiawatha*), 31,820 square miles. The Mackenzie, Canada's longest river, is 2,635 miles from its source to its Arctic estuary; the Yukon is 1,979 miles long, 714 of which are in Canada; the Fraser runs 850 miles to the Pacific.

Some of the waterways are still in use. The St. Lawrence system, ice-bound in winter, in summer supports a thriving merchant marine. Since the St. Lawrence Seaway opened in 1959, ocean shipping plies between the lake-ports and the great trading-centres of the world.

Newer communications have created new Canadas. The era of the bush pilots opened the North for exploitation of its rich mineral deposits. In the late 1920s and throughout the 1930s these incredible airmen pioneered the techniques of aerial mineralogical exploration. Flying their primitive machines over some of the most savage country in the world, compasses spinning crazily from closeness to the magnetic pole, they were often lost and sometimes killed. Sub-zero temperatures for which their engines had not been designed often forced them to thaw lubricating oil over stoves. Sometimes the oil caught fire. Sometimes the pilots were grounded for days and weeks in the bush, depending on their rifles and luck for survival. Because of what they learned, the two-fifths of Canada that lies outside the provinces is now more or less accessible. The Yukon Territory, the Northwest Territories, even the Arctic archipelago, are effectively bound to Canada.

The newest Canada of the automobile and the super-highway is still young. The Trans-Canada Highway runs with its connecting ferries all the way from St. John's, Newfoundland, to Tofino on the west coast of Vancouver Island. So far its effect, and the effect of other super-highways, has been to increase urban sprawl and hasten rural depopulation. In central Canada its by-passes have had the more pleasing result of allowing sleepy small towns to relapse, comparatively free of traffic, into their former complacent calm.

The speed-up of communications generally throughout the world has created what Marshall McLuhan (a Canadian) has called 'the global village'. A great deal of culture and popular folklore has become international. Perhaps in reaction, the late sixties saw a marked resurgence in regional nationalism in Canada as elsewhere throughout the world.

II

In theory, all the Canadas meet in Ottawa. In practice, the federal capital is merely a political centre, a romantic small city of trees, open space, and cascading water. The Gothic fantasy of Parliament Hill, dominated by its tall Peace Tower, looks over the chasm of the Ottawa River from English-speaking Ontario to the city of Hull in French-speaking Quebec. This hill is the nerve-centre of Confederation: the House of Commons with its British inheritance of mace, Speaker, and majority rule, and its North American 'omnibus' political parties; the rheumaticky Senate; the offices of the Prime Minister and the Leader of the Opposition as well as some of the great departments of a modern government. At a discreet distance,

Rideau Hall, with a heavy air of public works, houses the Governor General, who represents the Crown. Here, in the great gilded throne-room, foreign diplomats from the city's embassies and legations present their credentials. And from here, at the beginning of each session of Parliament, His Excellency sets out in all the glitter of vice-regal pomp with cavalry, coach, and plumed head-dress to read the Speech from the Throne in French and English.

The judiciary is present in the Supreme Court of Canada on Wellington Street: nine scarlet-robed justices, one of them the Chief Justice, who form the ultimate tribunal. Their work in hearing appeals is complex, for though there is a single criminal code for the whole country, there is a mass of purely provincial law – notably the civil code of Quebec, which is French in origin. Because appellants have the right to be heard in either official language at least four of the judges are French-speaking.

Ottawa houses other national institutions, fiscal, administrative, and cultural. Probably the most famous is the Royal Canadian Mounted Police. Tourists admire their scarlet tunics and the impeccable horsemanship of their famous musical ride. Reactionary but disciplined, the Mounties enforce the criminal code in eight of the provinces as well as in the Yukon and the Northwest Territories. In Ontario and Quebec, which have provincial police forces, the R.C.M.P. is responsible only for the enforcement of federal statutes other than the code.

Well over a third of Ottawa is directly engaged in government or political work. Like Washington it's a city of civil servants. Responsible, intelligent, and, sometimes, self-important, Ottawans talk political shop interminably.

In winter, its rivers locked in ice, the baronial extravagances of its public buildings stark against snow, Ottawa takes on a Victorian grandeur. Figures in dark topcoats and fur hats come and go with attaché cases, moving with the confident tread of men in power.

Yet though Sir John Macdonald, in drafting the British North America Act of 1867 which is still the base of Canada's constitution, sought to create a dominant central government, Ottawa's power to hold Confederation together is subject to heavy centrifugal strain.

In the 1960s an awakening French Canada is showing discontent with the old railway constitution.

Each province has its own lieutenant-governor, its own elected legislature, premier, and political parties, its own supreme court. Autonomous within the subjects of legislation reserved to them by the B.N.A. Act, the provinces are theoretically equal. In practice some are far more powerful than others. Quebec, as the guardian of French-Canadian language and culture, is more than a province. To many *Canadiens* Quebec is their nation.

More generally, the rich and populous provinces, Ontario and British Columbia no less than Quebec, seek to increase their autonomy. The weaker rely on a strong Ottawa.

III

There is no such town as Friendsville. But I can imagine it, a composite of Canadian dreams of small-town life. For perhaps no North American myth is more pervasive in Canada than this one of the friendly small town.

Approach by car; a sign at the town limits reads: 'WELCOME TO FRIENDSVILLE. Population 5,223. *Watch Out for Our Children*'. A second sign flashes, as it were, the municipal credentials – the badges of all the service clubs in town: Lions, Kiwanis, Rotarians, Oddfellows, Masons, Moose. Tall elms shade the street which in this part is residential. A few elegant old houses of wood-frame construction, painted white, sit well back from the sidewalk behind unfenced lawns. (To put up fences would be a sign of distrustful reserve.) On their gingerbread porches or verandas elderly ladies in rocking-chairs are knitting socks for charity. They watch fondly over their spectacles while small, freckled boys in tee-shirts and jeans hurry by with fishing-poles and cans of dew worms, heading for the creek. One of the ladies ('the girls' as they call themselves) has just baked a batch of cookies – 'as good as store-boughten cookies' – and is now on the alert for children to give them to.

Friendsville people get most of their pleasure from helping other people. As the Reeve puts it, 'Why, I'm just tickled to death to be able to do something for the other fellow.' Take Doc Murray, the general practitioner who lives over there in the pink clapboard ranch-bungalow – the one with the aluminum screen-door ornamented with the letter M. He never neglects a call, he's killing himself with work, yet he's so reluctant to collect bills that he hasn't had a new car for all of three years.

The centre of Friendsville is Main Street. There are several general stores, a hardware, a drugstore, the town 'character'. (Friendsville people are reticent with strangers about the character, but among themselves they enjoy stories of his drunken exploits.) There are two banks and three churches. In the short-order restaurant, run by a grumpy old Chinese with a heart of gold, there's a notice that says: 'Sunday Morning. A Fine Morning to Attend the Church of Your Choice.' A stout, smiling nymphet in a white coat two sizes too small hands the menu: the 'special' today is roast beef sandwich, french fries and cole slaw, home-baked apple pie. 'Will you have your beverage now or later?' she asks.

The myth has it that everyone in Friendsville knows everyone else, helps each other in trouble, is free of all snobbery and class distinction. Admitted that some are richer than others – the undertaker for one (or 'funeral director' as he prefers to be called) is palpably more prosperous than his neighbours – but no one is too grand to sit down to supper in the church basement with the folks. And all the business-men are working selflessly to attract industry to the town: it just seems wrong to keep such a delightful little place to themselves.

The life of Friendsville is charmingly set forth in Stephen Leacock's *Sunshine Sketches of a Little Town*, a portrait of his own Orillia, Ontario, in which every native Canadian discerns the features of his home town. The French-Canadian equivalent is a little different: here there is only one church, big and gaunt under its tin steeple, and the good-hearted townsmen are obedient, if critical, sons of *Monsieur le Curé*. But the essentials are the same: plain living and neighbourly hearts.

Probably most native Canadians have grown up in towns much like Friendsville. Nor is the myth very misleading. Small-town

Canadians are friendly, do help one another, and have managed to achieve something like a classless society. Yet if lawns are unfenced and doors hospitably open, small-town minds tend to be firmly closed. And though Friendsville's social distinctions are based on the comparatively harmless standard of money, they still exist. Because they live close together and know one another so intimately, Friendsville people feel watched and hunted. In defence they sometimes grow hypocritical and secretive.

The myth of Friendsville grew in an age when Canada was predominantly rural and agricultural. That age, like the era of the steam railway that gave birth to Confederation, has already passed into history. Yet the ghost of Friendsville lingers to haunt great metropolitan centres like Montreal, Toronto, and Vancouver, and to bring its warmth and furtiveness to the commuters in their exploding suburbs, the cliff-dwellers in their high-rise apartment developments.

Sign as you leave Friendsville: 'THANK YOU. COME AGAIN.'

Suburban life, with its coffee klatsches and neighbourhood parties, becomes a kind of affluent Friendsville. But there is one marked difference. Suburban subdivisions seem to be inhabited by people of a single age-group. If there are children on a street, it's unlikely that there will be any old people. Grandparents are a disappearing breed, at least so far as the young are concerned. The suburban family is being stripped down to its basic unit of father, mother, and children. The grandparents come from city apartments to call at week-ends.

Canadians are enthusiastic church members, and churches of all denominations are thriving social as well as religious centres. Perhaps it's fair to say that they are *more* social than religious. For in the suburbs the Puritan heritage of the small town undergoes a curious mutation: the obsession with what is morally right becomes an obsession with what is hygienic. Gluttony, for instance, is obviously no longer one of the seven deadly sins; it is simply unhealthy. (Perhaps in revolt against the dismal science of dietetics, Canadian adolescents consume vast quantities of potato chips and tooth-rotting soft drinks.) It is the same with the other deadly sins. They are not so much problems for the minister as for the social worker.

15

The friendliness of Friendsville survives in the city. Even in surly Toronto a man waiting in an icy wind for his bus is sometimes offered a lift.

IV

Canada is so intransigently regional that few generalizations about its national character are valid. All its citizens call themselves Canadian, yet the word means something different to each. 'Historically', Northrop Frye has said, 'a Canadian is an American who rejects the revolution.' This accounts for the descendants of the United Empire Loyalists, actual and spiritual, who fled the United States in order to continue living under the British Crown. It accounts, too, for those deeply religious French Canadians who reject the French Revolution. And it's true that both these groups have been influential in their own ways. An astute Canadian economist, Professor Harry Johnson of the London School of Economics, has written sarcastically of Canadian economic policy as having been 'historically dominated by the ambition to create a country rival in power to the United States, and so to prove that the Americans were wrong to revolt from colonial rule in 1776'. Yet many Canadians vigorously reject these negative traditions.

The truth is that the thought 'Canada' is impossible to think all at once. Love of country is difficult when, like Aristotle's 'creature of vast size – one, say, 1,000 miles long', its unity and wholeness are lost to imagination. And so the patriotism of Canadians tends to be – in a perfectly respectable and human sense – provincial, and even parochial.

The people of each region have their own character.

Maritimers are a seafaring race whose roots are deep in history. Canada is sometimes thought of (quite wrongly) as a 'new' country. The Maritime Provinces belong essentially to the Old World. The things that surprise, enchant, and sometimes distress North American travellers in Europe are also to be found here: craftsmanship, tradition, cheerful poverty. A sense of history clings about the silvery weathered shingles of fishermen's huts; the vivid colours of boats and lobster floats – red, blue, ochre, green – and the black-and-white dazzle of painted wooden houses are affirmations of life and vigour against the hard grey weather and the dangerous ocean. Men have been here a long time; they have come to terms with the forests, the rocks, the tides. It was in 1605 that Samuel de Champlain planted Canada's first settlement at Port Royal – now Annapolis Royal, Nova Scotia. Not far away, at Pubnico, there are some eight hundred French-speaking Nova Scotians named D'Entremont. Most of them have the ascetic features of the family face: they are all descended from the Sieur D'Entremont who landed here in 1650. St. John's, Newfoundland, was first settled in 1613: its people retain the Jacobean turns of phrase, the ballads, the hearty manners of their ancestors.

Maritimers, many of them with the quick pride of Scots Highland descent, are touchy about the chronic depression of their region. Aware that their economy is to some extent subsidized from central Canada, they resent 'Upper Canadians' and are fond of denouncing the frantic pace of life in Ontario compared with the pleasant, lethargic tempo of their own existence.

French Canadians cherish their own mythology and defensive folklore. 'Je me souviens', their motto, recalls the national trauma – the conquest of New France upon the Plains of Abraham before the walled city of Quebec. Since that fatal day, September 13, 1759, they have seen themselves as beleaguered champions of the Catholic faith and its guardian the French tongue in a continent predominantly American and Protestant. Henri Bourassa, most eloquent of Canadian orators, spoke for his nation when he cried out passionately at the Montreal Eucharistic Congress on September 6, 1910: 'Providence has willed that the principal group of this French and Catholic colonization should constitute in America a separate corner of the earth, where the social, religious, and political situation most closely approximates to that which the Church teaches us to be the ideal state of society. . . . But, it is said, you are only a handful; you are fatally destined to disappear; why persist in the struggle? We are only a handful, it is true; but in the school of Christ I did not learn to estimate right and moral forces by number and wealth. We are only a handful; but we count for what we are; and we have the right to live. . . .'

More than fifty years later the 'ideal state of society' of the devout *habitants* has disappeared and the French Canadians have become an urban proletariat. While the fragrant spirit of John XXIII sweetened their faith, they have discovered their political strength and a new sense of purpose. By a paradox they have become most sharply aware of their distinctness at the very moment when they are becoming most 'American'.

The crooked streets of Quebec City cast their old spell, delightfully French-provincial in the shade of old trees in summer, antique as a Christmas-card under winter snow. In the Citadel redcoats of the 22nd Foot wheel and stamp to orders shouted in the curiously nasal French of the province. *Monsieur le Président* (Mr. Speaker) sits under the crucifix in the Legislative Assembly. A spectacled nun appears at the grille through which visitors are interviewed at the ancient Couvent des Ursulines; a moment later she returns to display with shy pride the skull of General Montcalm. But such impressions can be deceptive. The dark-haired girls, demure in their little black dresses, are North American women, capable, energetic, adventurous. And under the sober jacket of the young *séparatiste* hurrying to early Mass beats the heart of an automobile salesman.

All this is much more obvious in Montreal, the world's second biggest French-speaking city. This is the city which, above all others, has seized the affection of Canadians. Novel after novel has explored the intricate life of its streets and parks. Despite the bilingual signs and the brooding presence of huge, prison-like religious institutions, Montreal is plainly a New World city. Everyone here is cheerfully on the make. There is that sense (strong, too, in Toronto) that nothing is permanent. Buildings are constantly being torn down to be replaced by taller and richer ones, streets being ripped open for new sewers or subways, ambulances racing to the rescue of accident victims, sirens screaming, signs dazzling, merchandise being sacrificed to make way for the new line, the new model, the new chain-store – the whole circus of planned obsolescence and competitive selling.

Expo 67, the world fair with which Canada celebrated its centennial year in 1967, was held in Montreal. All over the world it was acclaimed as a stunning success. All over Canada it excited national pride and euphoria. But for Montrealers it was especially satisfying. There was a grace and gaiety about the fair that was all their own.

French Canadians are awaking to the knowledge that this is their world and their country. They have recognized their enemy in the 'Anglo-Saxon' élite who dominate Canada's economy. This élite, though stoutly entrenched in Montreal, whose commercial life it controls, has its spiritual home in Toronto.

One of the few shared sentiments of all regions of Canada is an unreasoning dislike of Toronto. Unreasoning, because the Toronto loathed throughout Canada has pretty well ceased to exist. The dour, philistine Orangemen who earned the city its unpleasant reputation have long been outnumbered by swarms of immigrants from Europe and from other parts of Canada. True, there's still a great parade down University Avenue on the glorious Twelfth of July, with drums and bands and orange sashes and even King Billy on his white charger. But the crowds who turn out to cheer are mostly Italians – everyone, after all, loves a band. For if Montreal is bicultural, Toronto is multicultural – an expanding, expansive metropolis with a population of two million. As Montreal is the centre of French-speaking Canadian life, Toronto is the hub of English Canada. Here are centred its publishing and communication industries, its commercial and financial empires, music, art, and theatre. Heavy industry is close by in Hamilton, and a third of Canada's population is concentrated in the rich farmlands and small cities of southern Ontario within a radius of three hundred miles.

Ontario people are sober, hard-working, orderly; as if to insist on their difference from the Americans they resemble so closely, they are strong for the Queen. The men tend to be serious about their work to the point of solemnity; at the same time they cherish the image of Huck Finn and are boyishly eager to head out for the bush. They are decent people, if – as they often complain themselves – a bit dull. And they are not nearly so hostile to French Canadians as the latter had supposed. Reaction to separatism has taken the form of official bilingualism. French lessons are fashionable in the richer residential areas of the big cities.

The West begins at Winnipeg, a mystique of white Stetsons, 'man-size' beefsteaks, and back-slapping hospitality. There is a tendency, too, for the necktie to atrophy into a sort of halter of bootlaces. Ontario and Quebec and the Maritimes suddenly recede to a great distance not only in space but in time. Here they are 'the East'. The cities of central Canada, which seem to the people who live in them so new and raw, from here take on the aspect of ancient centres of privilege and decorum, crusted with culture and learning. Wide, empty landscapes of bald prairie, oppressed by the enormous sky, wait at the limits of prairie cities. The company of fellow-men becomes vital. And in Alberta, as the flat prairie begins to undulate in ever shorter and steeper waves to the foothills of the Rockies, the company of God himself is sought by the people of the 'Bible belt'; not only in theocratic colonies of bearded, black-clad Hutterites, but in churches and conventicles of innumerable fundamentalist sects.

British Columbia, cut off from the rest of Canada by range beyond range of enormous, uninhabitable mountains, lives its own life. British Columbians are the most American Canadians, furthest removed from bicultural compromises; they are also the most British. Life is pleasant in the mild green climate of the Coast. The mist comes down on the mountains and silent forests, the Pacific glimmers below – who needs Canada? 'As far as I'm concerned,' a British Columbian told me not long ago, 'the Atlantic Ocean might just as well be washing at the foot of the Rockies.' In the remote valleys of the Interior – as the hinterland of Vancouver is gallantly called – a few pilgrim souls, the last Puritans, live by the light of conscience: Quakers, anarchists, pacifists, the unhappy Doukhobor Sons of Freedom. Cowboys ride the range on the high, semi-arid plateau of the Cariboo country. Loggers, miners, and fishermen earn the provincial income. But most British Columbians are concentrated in the cities of Vancouver and Victoria where the living is easy, summer and winter.

People who do not know Canada sometimes think of it, as Voltaire did, as a few acres of snow.

It is, of course, a northern country. Over most of it the climate is one of violent extremes – swelteringly hot summers and Siberian winters. Arctic Canada – the true North – is almost uninhabited. There are only some eleven thousand Eskimoes. The other people of a few small, scattered communities like Churchill, Inuvik, and Aklavik live a frontier life with, at Inuvik, every modern convenience, including heated sewage. (Because of permafrost, drainpipes are above the surface, and have to be heated to avoid freezing.) Northerners regard the rest of Canada and indeed the rest of the world as 'Outside'.

There is still a powerful myth of the North. Against all evidence, Canadians sometimes like to think of themselves as a hardy, frugal race of *hommes du nord*. For the farther north one goes, the farther one is from the United States and from supermarkets, super-highways, and sleek-haired advertising-men in three-button suits. One must suffer to be a Canadian (says the myth): here incomes are lower and prices higher than in the republic to the south: go north, young man. Canadians may not be particularly hardy, but they are hard-headed. They indulge this dream only at election-time and when they are on vacation.

V

Canada is a society rather than a nation. Its coherence depends on a communications system in which the radio and television networks of the Canadian Broadcasting Corporation play a supremely important part. There is no central and controlling myth to focus Canadian diversity and foster its distinctness: the Crown, which in theory symbolizes the State, is an absentee landlord.

But there is one definitive doctrine that runs through the whole of Canadian history and life and into the remotest parts of Canadian territory. The doctrine of the panacea of compromise has almost the force of a myth.

By compromise the fierce debates between English and French, between Catholic and Protestant, between Church and State, between public and private ownership, between Ottawa and the provinces have been mediated or held in obeyance. In this way the peace has been kept between elements that are potentially hostile.

The great political parties, nominally Progressive Conservative and Liberal, are internally based on compromises so far-reaching that a Tory can easily be accommodated by the Liberals and a *laissez-faire* Liberal by the Conservatives. There is compromise everywhere. Should the railways be nationalized? Yes and no. Should there be commercial radio and television or a publicly owned system free of advertising? Yes and no. Is education the duty of the State or of the Church? It is the duty of both, of either and neither. Should murderers be hanged? No – that is to say, yes, depending on the circumstances.

By compromise Canadians manage to have the best of all possible worlds, and the worst. Canadians manage to live together peaceably by minding their own business and staying in their own backyards. No attempt is made to indoctrinate immigrants or children with State myths. It is enough that they respect the State and keep the laws. And there is little discrimination against anyone on the ground of colour, race, or creed.

But to mind one's own business may lead at last to lack of interest in other people. Canadians are little given to personal gossip. They get away from their fellows whenever possible to stare at lakes and trees and rocks. There are fewer good novels written in Canada (the novel being essentially concerned with Other People) and there is more good painting based on landscape than the country's state of civilization would lead one to expect. And the plight of some groups of Canadians – the Indians, for example, and the Negroes of Halifax County, whose condition is cruelly depressed – is bitter demonstration that the habit of live-and-let-live may become a kind of indifference.

And yet it is a good country, a state that has come into existence peaceably and maintained its integrity with remarkably little shedding of blood. Rich and resourceful, it is an open society in which power is decentralized, a free country that has remained innocent of

22

lawlessness and gang-rule. Hegelian ideas of the superiority of the State to the sum of its parts are so widely accepted that it may come as a surprise to find that here, where the State has become a sort of board of arbitrators, the human spirit flowers in quiet.

KILDARE DOBBS

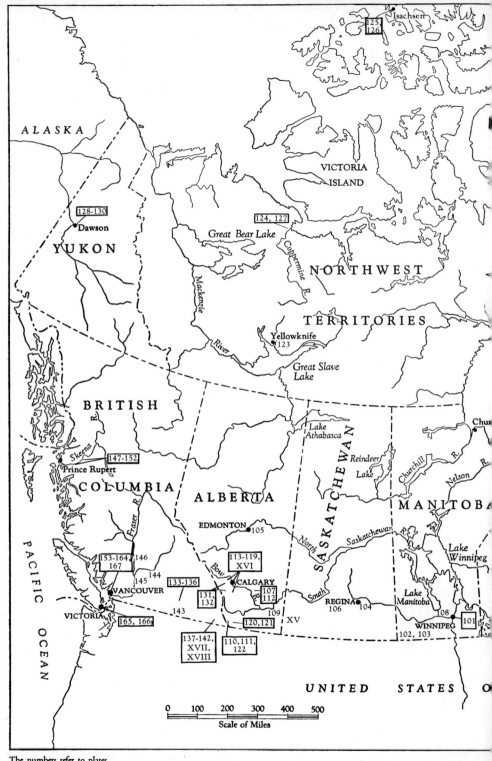

ALASKA

Isachsen
125
126

VICTORIA
ISLAND

128-130
Dawson

YUKON

Great Bear Lake

124, 127

Coppermine R.

NORTHWEST

Mackenzie

River

Yellowknife
123

TERRITORIES

Great Slave
Lake

BRITISH

Lake
Athabasca

Reindeer
Lake

Chu

Churchill R.

Nelson R.

Skeena R.

147-152

Prince Rupert

COLUMBIA

ALBERTA

SASKATCHEWAN

MANITOBA

Fraser R.

EDMONTON
105

North Saskatchewan

Saskatchewan R.

Lake
Winnipeg

153-164
167

146

113-119,
XVI

Lake
Manitoba

145

144

133-136

CALGARY

107
112

131,
132

109

Bow

South

REGINA
106

104

108

VANCOUVER

143

120,121

XV

WINNIPEG
102, 103

101

VICTORIA

165, 166

137-142,
XVII,
XVIII

110,111,
122

PACIFIC

OCEAN

UNITED   STATES   O

0   100   200   300   400   500

Scale of Miles

The numbers refer to plates.

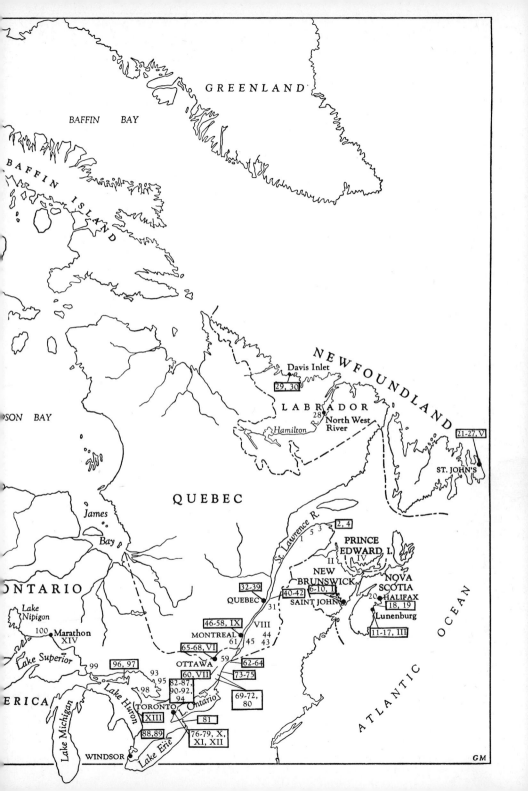

GREENLAND

BAFFIN BAY

BAFFIN ISLAND

HUDSON BAY

NEWFOUNDLAND

Davis Inlet
29, 30

LABRADOR

28 North West River
Hamilton

21-27, V

ST. JOHN'S

QUEBEC

James Bay

2, 4

PRINCE EDWARD I.
IV

II

NEW BRUNSWICK
6-10, II

NOVA SCOTIA
20 HALIFAX
Lunenburg
11-17, III

18, 19

St. Lawrence R.
1 5 3

ONTARIO

Lake Nipigon

100 Marathon
XIV

Lake Superior

99

96, 97

93

95

98

Lake Huron

Lake Michigan

AMERICA

TORONTO
XIII

88, 89

WINDSOR

Lake Erie

32-39

QUEBEC

40-42
31

SAINT JOHN

46-58, IX

VIII

MONTREAL
61 45 43

65-68, VI

59

OTTAWA
60, VII

62-64

73-75

82-87, 90-92, 94

L. Ontario

69-72, 80

81

76-79, X, XI, XII

ATLANTIC OCEAN

GM

THE GULF

1–5 The south shore and the Gaspé Region, forming the long lower lip of the ST. LAWRENCE RIVER, edge the river and the gulf in a smooth curve ending in the Baie des Chaleurs. It is all a rural, peaceful country, largely French-speaking, and poor through the Gaspé.

The little towns (such as Les Méchins, plate 1) straddle the road that runs for hundreds of miles within sight and scent of the St. Lawrence. About 400,000 people live

I LES MÉCHINS, Quebec

here in the settled strip, which is about 330 miles long and 30 to 80 miles wide. Inland are the hills, scarcely inhabited, rising to their peak at Mont Jacques Cartier, 4,160 feet. The names of the south shore and Gaspé are memorable: St. Jean Port Joli, Val Brilliant, Shickshock Mountains.

The centre of village life has for centuries been the church – in fact, the people think not so much of villages

27

or areas as of parishes. The steeples sheathed in tin or, lately, aluminum, shine over dozens of valley and seaside villages through the area.

Summer is Gaspé's great season: the painters, anglers, travellers, and politicians are back, talking and spending. The valleys shine, the weather is good, the roads passable. Winter is a yearly disaster. The storms close off the roads, and the men work for a pittance in the woods (sometimes not even earning enough to pay for the chain-saws they must buy), or else they go on relief. For weeks some of the backroads are plugged with drifts higher than the telephone poles, and the temperature itself seems frozen at twenty or thirty below zero F. Spring is as sudden as the stoop of a hawk, and violent: foundations and roads heave and buckle as four or five feet of frost come out; conflicting gales twist the pines; the hillsides shed tons of meltwater and rain into creeks throttled with ice; bridges collapse. But the people sigh with relief, make their maple syrup, and go fishing for the Gaspé salmon.

2 ST. YVON, Quebec

29

The photographs, taken in November, catch the country in a cool mood, the fields shaven, the roads not yet walled with their customary winter drifts, the creeks open. The villages, Les Méchins (plate 1), St. Yvon (plates 2, 4), Grande Vallée (plate 3), and Mont Louis (plate 5), lie around the north-east end of the Gaspé lip.

3 GRANDE VALLÉE, Quebec

4 ST. YVON, Quebec

5 HARBOUR, MONT LOUIS, Quebec

1 ST. JOHN RIVER VALLEY, New Brunswick

THE MARITIMES

6–10, I, II A happy country this, the NEW BRUNS-
WICK of settled traditions and habits, but one that has
suddenly had to face up to violent change. The relations
between French and English have changed radically in
the last few years, and with them forms of government
and taxation, approaches to schooling and bilingualism.

34

6 ST. JOHN RIVER VALLEY, New
Brunswick

The part of New Brunswick where the English pre-
dominate is here, along the St. John River and its broad,
peaceful valley and up around Sussex on the road to
Moncton, among long, wooded, rolling hills (plates 8,
9, 10). 'The St. John River country is old-fashioned,'
Hugh MacLennan wrote of this valley and its people;

35

II OYSTER TONGER, NORTHERN NEW BRUNSWICK

7 ST. JOHN RIVER VALLEY, New Brunswick

'it makes you think of the growing years of eastern
America before the pressures developed. . . . The happi-
ness associated with the St. John . . . proceeds from a life
closely entwined with the river and with woods which
are still wild and abundant with game: with family
farms, small towns, neighbourly villages and plain
people living with nature at their doors . . .' (plates 1,
6, 7).

The peaceful look of the land still underlines this truth,
whether in Peter Varley's sympathetic photographs or
in the magic realism of New Brunswick painter Alex
Colville, some of whose work is reminiscent of this shot
(plate 7) by Varley on the banks of the St. John River.

Along the coast, the talk is of superports for deep-
water ships that need a hundred feet of water under their
keels, but still you see the oyster tonger with the ancient
tongs for lifting oysters from the beds (plate 11), and
wood lobster-pots weighted with stones and tied with
twine.

8, 9, 10 FARMS NEAR SUSSEX, New Brunswick ▶

37

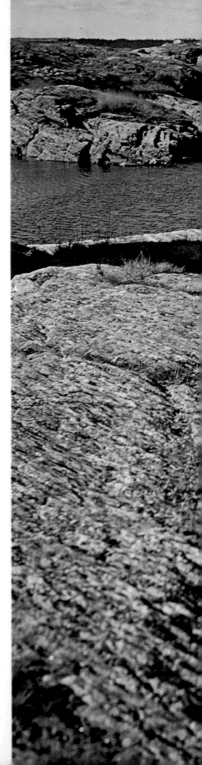

III BLUE ROCKS, SOUTH SHORE, Nova Scotia

11–20, III NOVA SCOTIA, sometimes characterized as an island joined to Canada by a narrow peninsula of resentment, has in fact given to the nation three prime ministers, many of the country's finest authors, and countless academics and businessmen. The province, like Britain and New England, the ancient lands of its people, is dented and cut by the sea: no part of it is more than forty-five miles from high tide. Lunenburg (plates 13, 15, 16, 17), along with dozens of other ports, coves, bays, and harbours round the coast, still sends its men to sea in ships. Nearly 8,000 men of this coast take their living from the sea, and supplement it with various forms of federal-government assistance.

Cove after cove along the south shore of Nova Scotia cuts into the land (plate III), and nearly every one has at its foot docks, dories, fish-houses (plates 12, 14), the strong smell of fish-guts rotting. Maybe a lobster-boat is in and the men are unloading. Then you can drive out on the dock (plate 11) and buy 'markets' – small lobsters – to take back to a fire on the shore. A dollar a lobster, and you need only some butter and a cool white wine to make an unsurpassable feast.

The accents of the people along the south shore are their own. The small town of Port Mouton west of Lunenburg is pronounced locally 'Port Matoon', and if you order your Chablis with the French pronunciation, the liquor-store man is likely to say, 'Around here that's Chabliss.' Perhaps uniqueness is inevitable, when the tongue must learn to cope with Shubenacadie and Musquodoboit.

11 UNLOADING COD, LUNENBURG, Nova Scotia

12 WOODEN LOBSTER POTS, South Shore, Nova Scotia

43

IV The red earth stains the melting snow and colours the road that runs through Hunter River, west of Charlottetown, on PRINCE EDWARD ISLAND. The clapboard church and houses, often white as in this photograph, are typical of Island architecture, at once elegant and simple.

Among provinces each as big as western Europe, Prince Edward Island is a sort of North American Andorra. Although her hundred thousand people live on an island smaller than many of Canada's lakes, they maintain the full apparatus of provincial self-government and send four senators and four members to Parliament in Ottawa.

Within a few generations after the land was settled, Islanders were hosts to delegates from Upper and Lower Canada and the other Maritime Provinces, beginning discussions that led to Confederation in 1867. The cautious Islanders stayed out until 1871, but in 1964 Charlottetown was the enthusiastic host for the ceremonies marking the one-hundredth anniversary of the conference. The city is also the site of the new Confederation Centre, a complex of library, theatre, art gallery, and museum, which commemorates the beginnings of Confederation.

45

The coaster (plate 15), built in Clarenville, Newfoundland, was designed to carry small loads of fish to
the West Indies, in an effort to expand Nova Scotia's
ancient but dwindling trade there. She is now used as a
cargo vessel round the Nova Scotia coast, carrying
package freight, coal, timber, and fish in bulk.

The sea that shapes the lives in the ports tempers the
climate all over the province. After the Pacific coast and
southern Ontario, Nova Scotia is the warmest part of
Canada. Halifax is, next to Vancouver, the wettest big
city in the country, with fifty-four inches of precipitation yearly, never less than three and a half inches in a
month.

St. John's Anglican Church (plate 17), founded in
1753, is entirely wooden. Wood has dominated Nova
Scotia – in the houses, the ships, even the graveyards,
where some of the headstones are in fact headboards
(plate 16).

14 DORIES, BLUE ROCKS, Nova
Scotia

46

Although some of the fishing-boats until recently were made with hand-adzed wood frames (plate 13) as they had been since before the American Revolution, the larger ones now are steel. The common food and export, salt cod, is unloaded from a Newfoundland fishing-schooner (plate 11) at a Lunenburg dock.

13 ADZING SHIP'S RIBS, LUNENBURG, Nova Scotia

15 COASTER, LUNENBURG, Nova Scotia ▶

16 FAMILY BURIAL PLOT, LUNENBURG

17 ST. JOHN'S CHURCH, LUNENBURG

This piece of Atlantic shore, the part of Canada closest to Europe, is also the part first permanently settled by Europeans (plate v, looking north past St. John's from Black Head, near Cape Spear). The first attempt to found a colony here was made by a company of Bristol merchants in 1503. Records of the colony are sketchy, and it apparently did not survive more than three years. St. John's was an important international fishing settlement when visited by Sir Humphrey Gilbert in 1583. Cupids, just to the north, was founded by royal patent in 1610. Bay Bulls, just south of here, was fought over furiously by English, French, and Dutch. Cannon left over from the ancient wars are used as gate-posts for the parish church.

Sir George Calvert, the first Lord Baltimore, planted a colony on this peninsula in 1622 and named the land Avalon. Baltimore's colony failed, but the name for the land remained Avalon. Baltimore later moved most of his colonists to Virginia, and Sir David Kirke, whose tomb is said to be somewhere near Ferryland, the site of Baltimore's colony, succeeded him. But Kirke, like all the other aristocratic planters, failed. Only the fishing settlements, founded without royal patent and actually in the face of stiff opposition from the British government, survived and flourished.

V SUGAR LOAF HEAD, NEAR ST. JOHN'S, Newfoundland

49

Chester in summer is as pretty a place as you would want to see when the sun shines. The village, streaming down the steep hill under its tall old trees, is quiet, except when a few teen-agers on holiday suddenly scream by *en route* to the new salt-water swimming pool, or else ride horseback down the main street. The houses retire gracefully under shady trees, the lanes curve between tall green hedges. In gardens beyond, voices quietly talk, or a woman's summer dress floats. The sleep of early summer afternoon, hot sun on a dusty road, the flashing sea – everywhere the peninsula and Mahone Bay are beautiful. The town looks out onto this scene (plate 18), Mahone Bay, where the yachts race in the summer afternoons, and the ferry crosses to Tancook Island, a low hump in the distance. Oak Island, home of wonderful rumours of gold, is only a couple of miles from shore here. In the summer, the south-west bay is quiet enough that you may even paddle a canoe on the ocean, among tall-treed islands and headlands (plate 19, town of Mahone Bay).

18 MAHONE BAY, Nova Scotia

19 TOWN OF MAHONE BAY

20 The centre of industry and transportation in Nova Scotia is its capital HALIFAX, and Bedford Basin (plate 20) with its tankers and warships is one of the busiest shipping areas in Canada (sixth in total tonnage in 1960). The city itself, foggy, old, and quiet, has lately been changing. A new automobile factory has been set up across the harbour at near-by Dartmouth; industry has expanded and found new markets; drama has had a revival under Canadian directors and playwrights. The old hopes of Nova Scotia are beginning to materialize in action.

20 HALIFAX HARBOUR, Nova Scotia

21–27, v Fishermen's wood houses stagger down the east ledge of Canada (plate 21) overlooking the harbour entrance of ST. JOHN'S, Newfoundland. The outlook here is quiet and hopeful. The people are not rich, but few of them are poor in the sense of lacking essentials of any kind. The air is clean, the views are magnificent, and a man with a boat is a man with good health and an escape from his depressions. It is completely appropriate that the tune of a favourite old Newfoundland reel is lively and happy. The words are:

> I'se the bye that builds the boat
> And I'se the bye that sails her
> And I'se the bye that catches the fish
> And brings them home to Li-zer.

The attitude is independent, and the tune is sassy. Most of the men who live in this section of St. John's, the Upper Battery, are fishermen, and 'Li-zer' is not only used to seeing her husband's long-liner go out after cod from the harbour entrance (plate 26) but is ready to help clean, cook, or sell the catch (plate 22).

St. John's is the oldest city in Canada, first settled by Bristol fishermen early in the sixteenth century, about one hundred years before the Quebec and Virginia settlements. French, English, Basque, and Portuguese used to fish the Grand Banks and shelter here. It was of this bay behind its famous headlands that the Sieur de Roberval wrote, in the *Voyages, Navigations, Traffiques and Discoveries of the English Nation*: '. . . wee could not reach Newfound lande, untill the seventhe of June [1542]. The eight of the month, wee entred into the Rode of Saint John, where wee founde seventeene Shippes of fishers. While wee made somewhat long abode here, Jacques Cartier and his company returning from Canada, whither he was sent with five sayles the yeere before, arrived in the very same harbour. . . .'

The fishermen of today's St. John's live in the Batteries – Upper (plate 21), Lower, and Outer – so named because guns used to be mounted here to defend St. John's and the harbour (plates 26, 27) against, at different times, Englishmen, Frenchmen, Spaniards, and pirates.

55

21, 22 ST. JOHN'S, Newfoundland

23 SIGNAL HILL, ST. JOHN'S HARBOUR, LOOKING TOWARDS CAPE SPEAR

57

24 SUGAR LOAF HEAD, ST. JOHN'S, Newfoundland

25 CABOT TOWER, ST. JOHN'S

Signal Hill (plate 25), where this stone ruin stands, overlooks St. John's Harbour, and is included in Signal Hill National Park. Here, in 1901, Marconi received the first transatlantic radio message, and here, during centuries before, Newfoundlanders watching for enemies approaching the harbour prepared to shell them from stone forts.

Near Sugar Loaf Head (plate 24), or the Sugarloaf, just north of St. John's, is a prime fishing-ground for long-liners from St. John's.

For all its apparent devotion to tradition, Newfoundland has changed profoundly since confederation with Canada in 1949. Fishing has shrunk in importance until it now accounts for only ten per cent of the island's income. Since 1949, schools with more than 5,000 new classrooms have been opened, 2,500 miles of new roads have been built, and 1,300 paved. Public health standards have been raised close to the national level and the increase in the *per capita* income has been among the fastest in the world.

Life has been imitating the artist in Newfoundland in at least one instance: forty years later, the province followed its great poet, E. J. Pratt, into Canada. Pratt, who graduated from Victoria College in Toronto in 1911, lived there the rest of his life, but his lyric poems are chiefly of Newfoundland – 'The Toll of the Bells' illustrates the sadness of the sailors' death:

> We gave them at the harbour every token –
> The ritual of the guns, and at the mast
> The flag half-high, and as the cortege passed
> All that remained by our dumb hearts unspoken.
>
> (From *Collected Poems* by E. J. Pratt.)

28–30 LABRADOR, to most Canadians, is a word like heaven, with a definite meaning – cold and barren – but no particular geography. They would like to see it, but the chances seem remote. They are vaguely aware of a long strip of land up the east end of the country, and some inlets. That is about all. From the point of view of Apartment Man, there is nothing more. He is happy to read about it incidentally in E. J. Pratt's lines in 'The Titanic', describing the birth and drift of an iceberg:

> Calved from a glacier near Godhaven coast,
> It left fiord for the sea – a host
> Of white flotillas gathering in its wake . . .
> . . . No smoke
> Of steamships nor the hoist of mainsails broke
> The polar wastes – no sounds except the grind
> Of ice, the cry of curlews and the lore
> Of winds from mesas of eternal snow;
> Until caught by the western undertow
> It struck the current of the Labrador . . .

This current, sweeping down from the Arctic Ocean, keeps coastal Labrador fog-free but frozen during most of the year. The settlements have a mixture of people: English–Scots immigrants whose ancestors arrived in the nineteenth century, Eskimoes, and Nascaupi Indians (plate 28, paddling out the North West River at Lake Melville near the settlement of North West River).

Part of the Algonkian group, the Nascaupi range over all the Labrador peninsula, from the St. Lawrence to Ungava, from Hudson Bay to the Atlantic. In the southern part, around settlements such as North West River, the caribou are nearly gone and the Indians have little to live on. They hunt in winter and fish in summer but the results are so poor that much of their food, clothing, and shelter is charity, given by the government of Newfoundland. The Indians also work as foresters, fire-fighters, and guides, and make the best fire-fighting teams the government has ever employed.

Like all Canadian Indians today, the numbers of the Labrador Indians are increasing, due to regular and proper medical attention, especially in infancy. Most of

27 BATTERIES FROM SIGNAL HILL, ST. JOHN'S, Newfoundland

the population is under the age of twenty. The Nascaupi canoes (plate 28) are made at home with wooden frames and wooden planking split out of round sticks from the forest. Imported canvas is stretched over the wooden hulls to make them watertight. The paddles are carved from spruce logs.

At Davis Inlet (plate 29) in north Labrador, the Nascaupi come to buy food and clothing. They use wooden one-cylinder putt-putts, largely made in

28 NASCAUPI INDIANS, NORTH WEST RIVER, Labrador

64

Toronto or Montreal. From these boats they fish for
cod, sea-trout, and salmon.

Joe Rich, Chief of the Davis Inlet bands, tells a story to
family and friends in his hunting tent (plate 30) set up
specially for the photographer. Hunting tents are usually
of caribou skin stretched on spruce poles, but this one
was made of old blankets and parachute silk. Spruce
branches hold down the floppy material, tied together
with strings made out of roots.

30 WIGWAM, DAVIS INLET

Used to walking long distances over their heavily forested country in search of game, these Indians, like their inland relatives generations ago, have an amazingly accurate sense of place. Any hunter can quickly draw a precise map of hundreds of square miles of his territory. Their powers of endurance are remarkable: they commonly cover forty miles in a day on foot, and one woman recently walked eighteen miles to have her baby baptized. It was three days old when she set out.

Inland from these people, Labrador is alive with the sound of helicopters and iron-ore trains in the mountains and river valleys. Engineers are building the world's largest power-house under a thousand feet of rock on the Churchill River. They expect to produce ten million horsepower of electricity, of which six million will be at Churchill Falls alone. Already the town of Sept Iles, just a tiny fishing village a few years ago, is the third largest port in Canada – only slightly smaller than Montreal and Vancouver – in tonnage handled. Virtually all its business is to or from the iron mines at Knob Lake on the Labrador–Quebec border, and the even larger iron mines at Wabush and Labrador City in south-western Labrador.

29 DAVIS INLET, Labrador

67

31 ST. LAWRENCE RIVER, NEAR QUEBEC CITY

32 HARBOUR, QUEBEC CITY

31–39 This part of the St. Lawrence, backed by long hills (plate 32), is perhaps the best-known stretch of river in Canada: it has certainly stirred the emotions of millions of immigrants, travellers, and returning Canadian soldiers, in sailing ships and liners, arriving to anchor here or passing up-river almost with the feeling of obeisance. The east windows of the turreted Château Frontenac hotel (plate 33) look over the Lower Town and harbour, over the Beauport shore (right) and Ile d'Orléans, the classic view from ancient QUEBEC. The hills to the north-east (background) are the beginning of a tremendous hinterland that stretches, lightly inhabited, to the Lake St. John country, and from there on, virtually deserted, to the shores of the Arctic Ocean at Davis Strait. If Quebec is the first sight of metropolitan Canada for the returning traveller on board ship, it is the last for the prospector, lumberman, or geophysicist heading into the bush and muskeg of northern Quebec.

33 CHÂTEAU
FRONTENAC, FROM CÔTE
DE LA MONTAGNE,
QUEBEC

34 LOWER TOWN,
CHAMPLAIN STREET,
QUEBEC

35 ST. LOUIS STREET, QUEBEC

Quebec City's pre-eminence in Canadian life is a
matter of prestige, antiquity, and sentiment: she has not
much larger industry except her governments – provincial and ecclesiastic. (Gross annual manufacturing in the
city averages $400 million.) Quebec is by Canadian
standards a middling city (the metropolitan area
included 357,000 people in 1961, seventh in Canada;
the city proper had 171,000, ninth in Canada), but it is
focus and symbol for French North Americans from
Louisiana to Ungava, and to many of the five and a half
million French Canadians it is more personal and more
important than Ottawa. This St. Lawrence aspect of the
French citadel (plates 31, 32) has inspired artists, including J. W. Morrice, who painted views of the Lévis ferry
about 1905. The streets – Champlain (plate 34), St. Louis
(plate 35), and St. Flavien (plate 38) – and the boardwalk

71

36 NOTRE-DAME-DE-
QUÉBEC, QUEBEC

37 RUE DE LA
FABRIQUE, UPPER
TOWN, QUEBEC

38 ST. FLAVIEN
STREET, QUEBEC

on the Dufferin Terrace (plate 39) have inspired novelists, notably Roger Lemelin, whose good-natured Lower
Town characters have assumed a place in French-
Canadian literature and folklore. Notre-Dame-de-
Québec (plate 36) and the Château Frontenac (plate 33)
are pre-eminent in the city, which, considering its early
founding, has surprisingly few ancient buildings surviv-
ing whole. Most of the old buildings were destroyed or
heavily damaged by fire or by artillery.

Notre-Dame-de-Québec is a basilica, dating from the
middle of the eighteenth century. The interior, theatrical
in its grandeur, was executed between 1780 and 1800 by
the Baillargés, a family of architects, sculptors, and
wood-carvers.

Quebec stands clearly superior in its own mind to
compromising, erratic, effervescent Montreal, and the
proof is partly in the purity and ancient form of its
French. 'Tabagie' in the sign over a tobacconist's
(plate 37) is a word unused in Montreal, where they
say 'Tabac'. Such modernisms are frowned on by the
purists of Quebec, who contend, with support from
educated Parisians, that the French language at the city's
Laval University is in a better state than French any-
where else in the world.

39 CITADEL AND BOARDWALK FROM THE CHÂTEAU, QUEBEC

40–45 SOUTH AND WEST OF QUEBEC CITY, stretching up the St. Lawrence, is a pocket of fertile land
bordered by mountains. Chiefly rural, with an increasing
number of secondary industries, the country, especially
in the Eastern Townships nearer Montreal, has been
taken up only recently by French settlers. They moved
out from the St. Lawrence shore during the mid-
nineteenth century in a colonization drive that was
partly competition with the English Canadians. Thus
the names all through here, though predominantly
French, are mixed: St. Hyacinthe, Cowansville, Disraeli,
Iberville – with aboriginal compromises such as
Mégantic, Memphramagog. But names prove little
except a mixed history – a town with an English name
may be predominantly French, and vice versa.

The settlers took with them their seigneurial attitudes
to land, and divided the country into strips marked by
snake fences made of the felled timbers. Behind these
ancient wooden fences (plate 40) there may stand a
micro-wave relay tower.

40 FENCES, ST. MICHEL, Quebec

41, 42 FARMS NEAR ST. MICHEL

43 LAKE MASSAWIPPI, EASTERN TOWNSHIPS ▶

Autumn comes early to the uplands near Quebec City, with overnight snows that melt at morning (plates 41, 42), but farther south, near the lakes and lower, the hardwood bush (plate 43) shines red, gold, and brown, for over a month. Among them, like the blackness of a photograph slowly appearing in the acid, come forward the green-black pines, spruces, and cedars.

77

'A hardwood copse in the Eastern Townships of Quebec in Indian summer can be compared to nothing else on earth, being itself an absolute. . . . After the first frost has turned ferns to brown dust and the birds have flocked south, the woods around my house in the country are filled with the living presence of silence.' (From *Scotchman's Return and Other Essays* by Hugh MacLennan.)

There is a moment in early spring that is exactly like this moment in fall: the air is still, the crows are squawking, the tree-shadows lie pale over a light ground. It was this moment in a copse such as this (plate 44) in the Eastern Townships that A. Y. Jackson painted in his *The Edge of the Maple Wood* (National Gallery of Canada), one of the most beautiful of all Canadian landscapes.

Cut-stone churches with tin roofs (plate 45) stand in scores of villages throughout this countryside. The wooden side-door is used on the coldest days in winter, when the front doors would be too draughty. These churches are closely related in style to the earlier buildings on the Ile d'Orléans near Quebec City: the church at Ste. Famille there, for instance, with its corner belfries, is an obvious precursor in style of this Eastern Townships specimen.

45 COUNTRY CHURCH, EASTERN TOWNSHIPS ▶

44 MAPLE WOODS, EASTERN TOWNSHIPS, Quebec

46–49, IX An impossibility that suddenly arose in the St. Lawrence, real and full of people: EXPO 67. Achieved, enjoyed, and then left behind like a summer picnic – in every stage Expo still seemed unreal. For all the wood and steel and concrete, Expo still had the shapes of a dream, the colours, arrangements, juxtapositions, and contradictions. Here a curved wooden ziggurat (plate IX, Man and the Community) or a monstrously expensive low-cost housing development (plate 48, Habitat) rose above the prosaic Montreal waterfront, the ziggurat lighted at night so that it glowed with the soft grain of its wood flanks. Here little trains rose high over canals where vaporettos hissed past (plates 46, 49). Curves, cubes, bubbles, triangles, thatched cones – every conceivable shape appeared somewhere in a building. The German tent stretched in hyperbolic paraboloid curves intersecting

46 MINIRAIL, NEAR SWAN LAKE, EXPO 67, MONTREAL

at tall steel poles (plate 47). The minirail gave ideas for transport at other, continuing exhibitions in Canada. What Expo did for Canada was incalculable. It was arguably the most important peace-time event in the history of the country after the building of the C.P.R.

Some critics have said that it gave Canadians confidence. Rather, it gave them a supreme chance to demonstrate existing confidence. And to show off in a hundred ways – something that Canadians are inclined to do much more abroad than at home.

Quebeckers, hosts to the show, were especially proud of Expo. In fact, Montreal mayor Jean Drapeau was so pleased with it that he defied the spirit of the international rules governing continuance of exhibitions and created an annual event from Expo. Ontario people went out from the Christopher Chapman movie *A Place to Stand* light-headed with pride in the beauty and power

47 GERMAN PAVILION, EXPO 67, MONTREAL

of their province (later Chapman's movie won an
Academy Award). Europeans from every country,
Americans from every state, were dazzled by the
splendour of this unknown Canada that leaped at them
or wooed them in scores of ways.

As Robert Fulford commented in his book *This Was
Expo*: 'That feeling – not only of accomplishment in
hand, but of even greater accomplishments to come –
lasted all through the six months of Expo's existence,
and among some of us it exists yet. It seemed to me to
mark the end of Little Canada. . . . We discovered our-
selves.' The public agreed, long after the event. When
Fulford's book went on sale, the publisher had to hastily
double the original print order to meet an unprecedented
demand. Even as a memory, Expo had power.

48 MONTREAL HARBOUR, HABITAT AT RIGHT, EXPO 67

49 FRENCH PAVILION, BEYOND MINIRAIL, EXPO 67

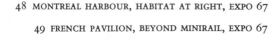

84

50–58 The words of the fine French-Canadian poet Saint-Denys Garneau frame one view of MONTREAL:

> I walk beside a joy,
> A joy which is not for me.

Different, but close, like the statue of CHARITY (plate 50) beside the citadel of commerce (Canadian Imperial Bank of Commerce Building), the elements of Montreal stream along side by side, seldom mixing. Catholic, Protestant, Jew; French Canadian, English Canadian, New Canadian; Separatist, Federalist – the tinctures of difference are unending. The area round Place Ville Marie is almost the only common ground – apart from the Forum, the Art Gallery, and the Symphony – where something does not divide one citizen from another. The newsboys and most of the salespeople here – on Dorchester (plate 52), St. Catherine (at Peel, plate 53), Rue de Vitre (plate 54), and Metcalfe (plate 52) – have an uncanny knack for telling a customer's language before he speaks, judging from a coat, a look, a haircut, perhaps even a man's gait.

Where the two cultures do touch intimately, however, there is likely to be the light and force of fusion. In certain regiments, including the Fusiliers Mont Royal, at both the great universities, Montreal and McGill, in the C.B.C. and the National Film Board, in the *boîtes*, and especially among painters and writers, there have been brilliant signs of the advantages of cultural disunity. The women of Montreal, benefiting from both cultures through marriage, ancestry, or friendship, are the most attractive and charming in the country.

Place Ville Marie stands cold, tall, and regular in the middle of the most valuable real estate in the city. The development covers seven acres of land, houses the head offices of several big Canadian enterprises, and has spurred development of other blocks downtown. Its inhuman regularity and size stand almost as if accused by the stone apostles on top of the Cathedral of Mary Queen of the World (plates 51, 56), seat of the Catholic Archbishop of Montreal.

88

◀ 50, 51 CHARITY AND COMMERCE, PLACE VILLE MARIE, MONTREAL, Quebec

53 PEEL AT ST. CATHERINE, MONTREAL

54 RUE DE VITRE, MONTREAL

Parc Lafontaine (plate 55), in the middle of the
French and *bourgeois* east end of Montreal, is usually
littered with students from the school that stands at the
south end of the grounds. The park, divided by the
Avenue Calixa Lavallée, contains a big track-and-field
ground in the east half, and a lagoon in the west,
complete with swans, bridge, and bun-eating ducks.

55 LAFONTAINE PARK, MONTREAL,
Quebec

56 CATHEDRAL OF MARY QUEEN
OF THE WORLD, MONTREAL

These gutters of traffic between immense curbs of stone and glass would have astonished the fur-hatted, fur-trading men who expanded the commerce of Montreal to a vast hinterland in the West. Not far from here (plate 54), to the east end of the Montreal business district, at Beaver Hall Hill, was built in the eighteenth century a log house eighty feet long by thirty-six wide. To its owner, Joseph Frobisher, came his Canadian partners and friends talking of the vast enterprise that traded or explored as far away as the Arctic and Pacific shores of the continent.

The country that these men opened and exploited is nearly all deserted now: modern Canada, following the east-west routes they pioneered from Montreal, has turned south from them to build her cities and farms. The original canoe routes west from Montreal followed

57 ST. LAMBERT LOCK, MONTREAL, Quebec

the southern boundary of the Canadian Shield all the way to the Athabaska territory, crossing the Shield at Lake Nipissing and at the Superior–Red River route. So important has this route been in history that most Canadians today still imagine that they are a Shield people, when in fact not a single one of the fourteen biggest cities stands on Shield rock. Most of those cities, such as Toronto and Vancouver, are far distant from the Shield; only two (Quebec and Ottawa) stand even within sight of the Canadian Shield hills. But large parts of the old trade routes are still in use: down the Great Lakes to Montreal, and thence across all the oceans. Much of the trans-shipping is at Montreal docks (loading grain brought east by rail, plate 58), but there is a large direct-freight traffic via the St. Lawrence Seaway (St. Lambert Lock, plate 57).

58 SHIPPING GRAIN, MONTREAL HARBOUR

59 FLOODED AREAS, ST. LAWRENCE SEAWAY, Quebec

60 BOATHOUSE, RIDEAU CANAL, Ontario

61 LACHINE RAPIDS, ST. LAWRENCE SEAWAY

59–61 Standing waves of white water face up-stream in the Lachine rapids (plate 61), along the Montreal river-front. They were first bypassed in 1825 by a canal with seven locks and a depth of five feet. Today, the SEAWAY CANAL along the south shore from Montreal to Caughnawaga is twenty miles long with two locks whose minimum dimensions are 766 feet (length) by 80 feet (breadth) by 30 feet (depth). The construction of the Seaway and the accompanying hydro-power developments meant the flooding of large areas (plate 59) between Lake Ontario and Montreal. From the air can still be seen the outline of old highways and canals under the water. This destruction of settled lands in eastern Ontario, part of the area called by pioneers 'the Front', prompted the Ontario government to move or reconstruct and restore historic old houses in its Upper Canada Village near Morrisburg (plates 62–64).

An earlier wave of canal-building, prompted not by commercial necessity but by military needs, resulted in the joining of the Ottawa River with Lake Ontario via the Rideau and Cataraqui rivers in 1832. Together with locks on the Ottawa, the Rideau Canal (plate 60) provided between Montreal and the Great Lakes a water route safer from American attack than the direct St. Lawrence passage. Soon after 1832, however, the British-American rivalry in North America had passed out of the military stage, and the Rideau has since become an attraction for tourists in cabin cruisers, many of them Americans.

62–64, VI, VII

All men love the old house, roofed with brown,
  Rising grayly from its woodland ring,
Over all the valley, ford and town,
  Facing westward like an agèd king . . .

Into silent glades and leafy places
  Footsteps follow where the quiet flies –
Sunlight scattered upon restful faces
  Shadows fallen upon pensive eyes. . . .
  Voices sweet
    Ebb and flow:
  Quiet feet
    Come and go
And among the faded stalks and ruined roses
The easy master of the house reposes.
          (From *The Poems of Archibald Lampman*.)

Lampman has expressed part of the reason why the Ontario government was concerned about the destruction of ancient homesteads, churches, and houses during construction of the St. Lawrence Seaway. Buildings from the areas to be flooded were brought with a variety of others to make a village near Morrisburg with streets, mill, river – an atmosphere of its own – in the style of 1867. The houses are in clapboard (the French/Robertson house, plate 62), vertical siding, dressed stone (the Loucks house, plate 63), locally made brick, and squared logs (the hired man's house, plate 64). The buildings date from 1784 through the nineteenth century, but most have been restored to 1867 or a little before.

The French/Robertson house (plate 62) was built by Jeremiah French, who left Vermont about 1786 and built his first house here of frame. Later it was extended, and covered in clapboard. In front is an early door-yard garden. In the words of an early Scots gardener in Ontario: 'My flowers are very fine hollyhocks grown from seed I brought with me. Mignonette fills the air with sweetness, a grove of fine sunflowers and scarlet runners is in front of the house. I assure you it looks quite gay. . . .'

62 FRENCH/ROBERTSON HOUSE, UPPER CANADA VILLAGE, Ontario

63 LOUCKS HOUSE, UPPER CANADA VILLAGE

The garden of the hired man's house (plate 64) is extensive. Behind the three-rail, double-post-and-yoke fence are lilac, yellow burnet, rose, and pelargonium, among many other flowers. Behind the house is a large vegetable bed. The tree at right, an apple, is just finishing bearing, and the young whip before the left-hand window has recently been transplanted. A sheaf of drying corn frames the photograph on the left.

The eavestroughs of the house are made of wood, and the chimney and fireplace are of stone. Typically, these houses had a kitchen, a living-room, and two bedrooms downstairs, with a sleeping-loft above. Inside, this house is plastered and papered.

The Loucks house (plate 63) did not have fireplaces (note chimneys) but was heated by stoves, with a complete system of immense heat holes in the inside walls to circulate the warm air. There is a storage basement under the house, from which a dumb-waiter ascends to transport the cooled foods upstairs.

98

65–68, VI To these old buildings, men in beaver hats come to legislate. Their breath smoking as they cross from the Chateau Laurier hotel (next to the East Block of Parliament, from which plate 65 was photographed) after dinner for the evening debate, they have a moment's dark resemblance to their ancestors and predecessors, who paddled the Ottawa River (in the background) to buy beaver for fur hats. The shapes around them, the stone walls that echo their feet stamping off the snow, are older than the nation they govern.

The cornerstone of the first PARLIAMENT BUILDING was laid in 1860 by Edward, Prince of Wales. It was in a style similar to the romantic style of the West Block (plates 65, 66, left, 68), and there were drinking- and smoking-rooms for the M.P.s. Then the fire of 1916 destroyed the roof, floors, and parts of the walls of the original Centre Block. It was rebuilt, but in a simpler and more august style. The smoking-rooms, the drinking-rooms, and the fancy vanished together. Government buildings today, like government itself, are bigger, cleaner, and less imaginative than under Victoria. Hardly an architect in the world today would dare design something as frilly as the final (plate 65), shaped in wrought iron like a fleur-de-lis, or the fussy, typically mid-Victorian iron cresting atop the West Block (plate 68).

The Centre Block itself is a sizeable but not over-powering building. The proportions of the original tower were improved in the reconstruction (designed by John Pearson) and a storey was added. There are now 490 rooms in the building, which measures 470 by 235 feet. The tower, 291 feet high, carries a fifty-three-bell carillon.

The Library of Parliament (plate 67, and behind the Centre Block, to the right, in VI), which was saved

65 WEST BLOCK,
PARLIAMENT BUILDINGS,
OTTAWA, Ontario

66 PARLIAMENT
BUILDINGS, Ottawa

from the 1916 fire by an iron door in the corridor, was itself damaged by fire in 1952 and then restored. It was inspired by the Gothic chapter-house – the style is an over-elaborated example of Middle Gothic, especially on the exterior. Normally, the circular shape is not successful for a library, although two famous circular libraries – the British Museum Reading Room and the Radcliffe Camera at Oxford – continue despite the inherent difficulties of noise and cramped stack space.

68 OTTAWA SKYLINE
FROM WEST BLOCK

VII COUNTY ROAD, RIDEAU LAKES,
NEAR OTTAWA

69–72, VII The countryside south of Ottawa, now dry and slow with late summer, is too hot for field-work in the early afternoon, and all the farmers take an hour's siesta in the hammock on the lawn after dinner.

Beyond them are great elms and poplar trees
That guard the noon-stilled farm-yards, groves
   of pine,
And long dark fences muffled thick with vine . . .

That was Lampman's description of a countryside like this in the 1890s. The roads are wider now, but the elms still stand over them.

The great gift of the super-highway in Ontario is not fast travel but empty sideroads, like this gravel road in the Rideau countryside (plate VII). Well kept through the whole year, except for a couple of dishevelled weeks in spring, roads like these now wind beautifully for many thousands of miles through farming and lake country, edged with maple or elm trees growing golden in the long, warm autumn. A snake fence of interlocking split rails, which undulates like a snake's progress, is hidden in the growth of maple vines to the right, and ahead, the trees over the road, as in many places, are so dense they form a tunnel of leaves.

In the fall the sumacs (plate 70) are among the first to turn, becoming an incredibly vivid red, which they hold for months, in great swathes and heaps of colour over the dry grass. The barns (plate 71) are typically hip-roofed and, by this season, loaded with carefully mowed hay, usually timothy. This crop is followed often by a second crop, alfalfa, which grows below the hay in the same field and is harvested later. This year's thrashing is over and the baled straw is stacked outdoors in the barnyard to the left. The hardwoods here (plate 72), photographed in September, are beginning to show the contrasts of autumn; the milkweed pods (at fence) are loaded with seedy, soft down.

Old habits linger among the farmers. Many of them keep unneeded horses in the barn although they have tractors and cars in the drive-sheds, and you will hear them refer to the 'hind' wheels of their cars.

69 VINE AND ROCK, Ontario

70 SUMAC, Ontario

71 NEAR LANSDOWNE, Ontario

72 AUTUMN FIELD, GANANOQUE, Ontario

106

In the pale days of early March, the snow shrinks back from woodpiles (plate VIII) and southern slopes. Soon the city people return to see how their cottages weathered the winter. Villager and city man shake hands, survey the sky, talk about the snow. Logs cut the previous fall, like these, may be hauled from the dripping pile to throw on the fire under boiling maple sap. Or if they are for the fireplace, they may best be split now while still frozen: when the frost is in the wood, the logs split at a single blow of the sledge-hammer on the wedge. About now, or a little later in the year while the sap still runs, you may cut maple trees. The logs, cut with sap in, burn with a blue-edged flame and a sweet, strong smell.

VIII MAPLE LOGS, EASTERN TOWN-SHIPS, Quebec

IX MAN AND THE COMMUNITY,
Expo 67, Montreal

73 VICTORIAN HOUSE,
BROCKVILLE, Ontario

74 CITY HALL, BROCKVILLE

75 STONE CHURCH, BROCKVILLE

73-75 Three buildings from the BROCKVILLE of the late nineteenth century show the taste of the Canadian Loyalist and Scots builders for medieval fantasy (note the spires of the church, plate 75; tower of the house, plate 73) and for the English Baroque. The church is a fairly characteristic example of late-Victorian Gothic. The limestone walls are rockface (that is, finished roughly, with an artificial bulge to simulate natural rock, in the manner of the Greek rustication). The City Hall (plate 74), built in the fifties, is relatively smoothly dressed and shares with many Ontario public buildings of the time the influence of the English Baroque. The upper walls are hammer-dressed, and the basement and portals are rockface. The outline of the cupola is slightly Baroque, and a purist would probably insist that the clock-faced dormers are too large for the building.

The house (plate 73) was probably built about 1870-80 and is eclectic medieval in style. This style was extensively used, in wood, for summer cottages in the Thousand Islands area of the Upper St. Lawrence River, near by.

111

76–80, x A first-class orchestra with a brilliant, talented and charming Japanese conductor; dark old businessmen's clubs where old-crony members play English and Russian billiards every day at noon, lunching on scotch and sandwiches. A city with a million recent immigrants from round the world. A city that has no Playboy Club, and showed the movie *Ulysses* uncut; an amusedly tolerant place which has long had anti-discrimination laws and segregated clubs and which has recently elected more Jewish than Orange Lodge mayors.

A city of poets and musicians, scientists and doctors, whose sons have won two Nobel prizes (Medicine and Peace), whose premier novelist, once part of the old Paris mob that included Hemingway and Fitzgerald, now lives in an old house on a shady street, writing good books long after the others have died.

Without boasting, virtually without realizing it, TORONTO has become the capital of Canada. So preoccupied with its own projects has it been that the people have scarcely realized that they have already developed the free, open, and creative sort of society envisaged by Prime Minister Trudeau as the shining future for this country. The city politics are democratic; its art is alive with the future and as modern as split-screen film; its immigrant aldermen head the fight for good government and reduction of urban blight. Its commuter system is ahead of all others in North America. Some of the brightest film-makers in the world are from this town.

Why?

The only possible answer is that Toronto is very sure of itself. It has plunged into the future in a manner that would have been reckless if it had not succeeded so fast. The world architectural competition for the new city hall, which resulted in Viljo Revell's unique design (plate x), was an example of daring that succeeds. From it have flowed other benefits – Nathan Phillips Square, the redevelopment of Queen Street immediately to the south, the purchase of Henry Moore's *Three Way Piece Number Two*, familiarly called 'The Archer' (plate 79), which stands directly before the tall curving Revell towers. As dusty a board as ever convened, the Toronto

X TORONTO CITY HALL,
COUNCIL CHAMBERS IN FOREGROUND

XI DOORWAY, ROSEDALE, Toronto

116

Harbour Commissioners, suddenly seized with the opportunities its waterfront land offered, proposed the most daring development scheme this or any other North American city had ever known. The sober commissioners proposed seriously that Toronto create artificially a charming complex of islands along its waterfront to accommodate a new airport and apartment space. The city, which had changed the existing Toronto Island into a long graceful waterfront park laced with lagoons, canals, and curved bridges, was enthusiastic about the idea. It would add miles of waterfront lined with trees, like this canal on the existing island (plate 78). Communications from the mainland would be by helicopter, boat, or subway.

78 TORONTO ISLANDS, Ontario

79 'THE ARCHER', BY HENRY MOORE, NATHAN PHILLIPS SQUARE, TORONTO

All this sprang from an old town typified in Rosedale (plate XI, a doorway in winter) and Kensington Market (plate XII). From the heart of supposedly Tory Rosedale and its companion Anglo-Saxon areas of the city recently have come novelists, playwrights, Academy Award-winning film-makers, painters, and pop-music composers of rare quality. The very symbol of change is perhaps here (plate 77) off Jarvis Street, where students of the National Ballet School rehearse on a hot July day with the door open. Their strict dance is casually watched by lounging sightseers who wander by from the near-by C.B.C. TV studios. Perhaps a producer shaded under the big old elms glances in at a future star dancing in this Friends' Meeting Hall where Quakers used to gather. Not all is change, however; reverence, restoration, preservation quietly keep good old ways and customs intact. The north end of the St. Lawrence Hall, encompassing the old indoor farmers' market (plate 76), has been rebuilt and restored to its original mid-nineteenth-century perfection. To this market every Saturday year-round come farmers from all around Toronto selling such country treasures as locust-blossom honey, fresh lake trout, newly pressed cider.

XII KENSINGTON MARKET,
TORONTO

80 KINGSTON, on the site of the ancient Fort Frontenac, outpost of the early French régime in Canada, has been fort, fur-trading post, naval base, legislative seat, and university town. Here, built on Point Frederick on the east edge of the city and viewed over the martello tower of the old Fort Henry (plate 80, below), is the Royal Military College. Founded in 1875, the College now trains officers for the combined services. It is built mainly of Kingston limestone. The towered stone building at right is the headquarters of the College; at

80 ROYAL MILITARY COLLEGE, KINGSTON, Ontario

the left, the building with the porch near the water (Deadman's Bay) is the old 'stone frigate', built long before the College for naval stores. Just projecting above the building next left is the top of a stone martello tower at Fort Frederick, similar to the one at Fort Henry. The nearer tower is thicker on the seaward side than on the landward, so that, if threatened with capture, the defenders could turn their cannon and blow out the landward wall, making the tower, for all intents and purposes, useless.

81–87 NIAGARA FALLS is, in strictly physical terms, a limestone ledge with fresh water falling over it. To most Canadians who live in its fall-out range, Niagara is the magnification of a cliché, although it may well provide their way of life, through its tourist industry or electricity. Yet in the very magnification, the falls are unique. The spray and pound of the falling water is oceanic; the frozen floes crouched over the fall's edge are like Labrador icebergs. The distance from shore to shore is 1,000 feet, the height of the falls 162 feet, the hydro-electric development on the Canadian side alone over two million horsepower.

The ways that Canadians have devised to provide views of the falls are so numerous and various that they are funny: there is a pair of little boats, each named *Maid of the Mist*, that bob around in the Whirlpool Rapids right under the falls; you can take the Scenic Tunnel trip, dressed in slicker and rain-hat, down through the rock to the Observation Plaza, and stare powerlessly at the water bursting out of the river above your head; you can edge along the river on an aerial buggy suspended on cables above the gyrating water of the Whirlpool Rapids, or on the little wooden foot-bridge by the river at the Whirlpool Rapids. You can fly over the falls in a little plane, or in a helicopter; you can go up a tower 325 feet high overlooking the falls, or like some of the local daredevils you could get into the traditional barrel and fall over the falls. Even barrels may go out of style: in 1961, Roger Woodward, aged seven years, wearing a life-jacket, fell into the river and was swept over the Horseshoe Falls. He was picked up in the whirlpool below, alive and well.

The water cascading over the Horseshoe Falls (plate 81, seen from the Seagram Tower) is of basic importance to one of the richest, most bountiful parts of Canada, a long peninsula of land jutting west from the line Toronto–Midland. Lake Ontario, Lake Erie, Lake Huron, Georgian Bay, and Lake Simcoe surround this section of low hills and fertile plateaux, making it almost an island, keeping it mild in winter, relatively cool in summer, and moist through the long growing season (at Windsor, 220 days). West from Toronto to Sarnia runs a climatic-botanical line of immense importance to

126

◀ 81 HORSESHOE FALLS FROM SEAGRAM TOWER

82 HOCKLEY VALLEY, Ontario

83 CALEDON HILLS, NEAR ALTON, Ontario

the whole nation, the line that divides the typical Canadian mixed forest zone to the north from a peculiar area called the Carolinian zone. In this large zone (approximately 22,000 square miles – twice the size of Belgium) many of the indigenous plants and trees are subtropical. The Carolinian zone, which extends through Mississippi into Louisiana, is named from the Carolinas of the United States, where it is best developed. In Carolinian Ontario the indigenous herbaceous plants include the Lotus flower, May apple, wild yam vine, and prickly pear. The trees include sassafras, paw-paw, sycamore, magnolia, Kentucky coffee, and red bud or Judas tree. These are the ornaments of a climate that supports orchards of apricots, pears, peaches, and apples, vineyards of wine and table grapes, fields that yield two or three fodder crops in a year, and, formerly, big groves of hardwoods (black walnut, curly maple, black cherry), which the pioneers of the nineteenth century converted into magnificent furniture. The men who opened this land to cultivation found flocks of wild turkeys, which were common in the eastern and southern States but unknown elsewhere in Canada.

The frost-free season at Point Pelee averages 197 days, only two weeks shorter than Vancouver's, and three weeks longer than Penticton's, in the fruitful Okanagan Valley of southern British Columbia. The waters draining away through Niagara help to keep this climate mild, for, when the cold fronts sag south over the continent in the winter, they come from the north-west and must pass over Superior, Michigan, Huron, and Georgian Bay to reach this land, and they are warmed in the passing. The influence of Lakes Ontario and Erie spreads north miles inland, keeping frosts short.

A little north of the richest belt, the country rises through a plateau into rolling hills (plate 83), and there the climate is sterner. Yet the Scots, German, and Loyalist pioneers clearing the land found it fertile and built their rail fences round fields that produced wheat bountifully. The stook of wheat or other grain (plates 84–87) is not so common, especially since the combines have invaded Ontario fields. These fields produced more wheat than any other area in Canada up to about 1915, when the West overtook them. Old

128

85, 86 COLLINGWOOD HILLS

87 DUNDALK PLATEAU, Ontario

methods have lingered longer here than on the great spreads of Saskatchewan (plate 84, forking up stooks of oats by hand). The farms helped to create an industry in farm machinery that grew up behind tariff walls, then branched out successfully to Europe, South America, and Asia. The horse-drawn Massey-Harris reapers, binders, thrashing machines, rakes (plate 85) are cast aside now, and the submarginal land, too, has been reforested (plate 82).

88–89 The people of STRATFORD, Ontario, used to their Romeo and Juliet schools, their River Avon, and Gad's Hill, decided impetuously in 1953 to give to their 'airy nothing a local habitation and a name'. Prompted by a local dreamer named Tom Patterson, they called in Alec Guinness, Tyrone Guthrie, Tanya Moiseiwitsch, and a tent-maker to make them a Shakespearian Festival. Now, the Festival is housed in a magnificent theatre built round the original stage (plate 82) designed for the first tent-theatre by Tanya Moiseiwitsch. It has presented Shakespearian comedies, histories, and tragedies, but has ventured further, with *Oedipus Rex*, *Cyrano de Bergerac*, original Canadian plays, light opera, Bach concerts, film and book festivals, and touring companies that have played Shaw and Marlowe in high-school auditoriums in Canada and theatres in North America and Britain.

Many Canadian players have gone from Stratford to Broadway or the West End, including Frances Hyland, Christopher Plummer, Kate Reid, and John Colicos. Irene Worth, Alec Guinness, and Siobhan McKenna have acted here, and great Canadian musicians have given concerts on this stage, among them Glenn Gould and Lois Marshall. From the start, Stratford has been first class, and today's companies are still developing fine new talents. Martha Henry rehearses *Troilus and Cressida* (plate 88) with Douglas Rain (Ulysses), Peter Donat (Troilus), and Len Birman (Diomedes).

Garrick Hagon (Patroclus; under stage balcony, plate 89), Leo Ciceri (Achilles; cloaked, centre stage), John Colicos (Hector; in cape, facing Ciceri), and Peter Donat (helmet, front right) rehearse *Troilus and Cressida*, which was designed by Desmond Heeley, directed by Michael Langham, and presented in 1963.

88, 89 'TROILUS AND CRESSIDA',
STRATFORD, Ontario

90 HARDWOOD BUSH IN MARCH, Ontario

91 APPLE ORCHARD, COLLINGWOOD, Ontario

90–92 Along the southern edge of Georgian Bay (near COLLINGWOOD, plate 92) is a region of high hills loaded with snow almost four months of the year, and supporting medium-length ski runs (plate 92, maximum vertical drop: 800 feet). The orchards from Collingwood (plate 91) to Owen Sound are all apples: stone fruits will not thrive this far north, although grapes do, wild and cultivated.

A March day in the woods here can be beautiful beyond imagination (plate 90). Working round the woods gathering maple syrup while the sun shines and the creeks begin to run, you feel the strength of the sun reawakening life, in the blood, in the sap of the trees pinging into the steel pails. Lampman expressed such a day in his poem 'Winter-Break':

All day between high-curded clouds the sun
Shone down like summer on the streaming planks.
The long bright icicles in dwindling ranks
Dripped from the murmuring eaves till one by one
They fell. As if the spring had now begun,
The quilted snow, sun-softened to the core,
Loosened and shunted with a sudden roar
From downward roofs.

132

93 ICE CRACK

93–95 To catch a whitefish, view the day, or shovel snow from a threatened summer-cottage roof, men walk out on the ice of GEORGIAN BAY (near Parry Sound, plates 94, 95) which, at mid-winter, is often frozen to a depth of four feet. Where the snow does not cover it, the hard blue ice has a beauty of its own: when pressure cracks appear (plate 93) in transparent fields, or on a day when a bay, though frozen, appears quite open. This happens when a thaw sets in after an early freeze, and the ice melts into little white balls, rounded by wave action. Then on a still, cold night the water re-freezes, the ice between the white balls dark and clear, so that the balls appear still to be floating on the surface, though in fact the ice is six inches thick around them.

A peculiar vehicle has been invented to traverse this ice. It is called a scoot, and it is about fifteen to twenty feet long, with a metal, toboggan-shaped bottom, and

92 DEVIL'S GLEN, COLLINGWOOD, Ontario

an aeroplane engine and a propeller caged on top of the rear section with an air-rudder behind. The faster scoots can do up to about 100 m.p.h. over ice. Carrying two to four people in a cabin, they can cross slush, open water, ice-floes mixed in water, sheer ice, and snowed ice. They are invaluable among the cloud of islands along the east coast of Georgian Bay, for without them the Indians and white cottagers could not travel during six to ten weeks of winter.

95 SHAWANAGA, GEORGIAN BAY, Ontario

94 ICE SHOVE, THORNBURY, Ontario

96–98 Like a huge limestone dock jutting out between Georgian Bay and Lake Huron, the BRUCE PENINSULA stretches north-west, covered with tourists and farmers (plate 98). The Bruce supports wild flowers rare in Canada, including the hart's-tongue fern and many varieties of orchid, among them the Alaska. So precious are the flowers that the Ontario government posts stern signs warning everyone not to pick them. No part of the Bruce is more than ten miles from the lake, hence the seagulls by the tractor (plate 98).

Farther north, on MANITOULIN ISLAND, the same limestone recurs. The people here are quiet, and proud that it was 'The Manitoulin', as they call it, that Lester Pearson represented when he was Prime Minister of Canada and leader of the Liberal Party. Progress has been missing here: today the people farm almost as they did one hundred years ago when the island was settled. They still use the squared-log barns (plate 97) and all-wooden snake fences, here not only being renewed but built new. Around enormous boulders of granite far too big to move (plate 96) the pastures run, and their fences in places may be walls of rocks laboriously picked and carried one at a time by generations of farmers bent to their land. Tractors are not new here, but some of the farmers still do not have one; they plough behind horses. Nearly all the other farmers keep horses, too, because they can get through the island's deep winter drifts when tractors fail.

138

96 GRANITE AND PINE,
MANITOULIN ISLAND, Ontario

97 SQUARED LOG BARN,
MANITOULIN ISLAND

99 LAKE SUPERIOR PROVINCIAL PARK, Ontario

99–100, XIV This is the SHIELD (variously named Pre-cambrian, Laurentian, and Canadian), which formerly was so important to Canadian life that the whole nation was shaped and nourished by it. Its furs, forests, and waters were the nation. Almost the only, and certainly the earliest, parts of Canada explored and settled by Europeans were in the Shield, or dependent on it for trade-goods. The country still depends on the woods for paper. (Canada produces forty-five per cent of the world newsprint total, and paper pays more wages in total than any other industry in Canada), on the rocks for minerals (asbestos, iron, nickel), and on the rivers for hydro-electricity. But few people live in the old North now: from being a relatively populous and civilized part of the country, it has changed to the emptiest and most primitive.

The hemlock and spruce in the foreground are typical of the great forests stretching north from this Superior shore (at Lake Superior Provincial Park, plate 99; near Marathon, plates 100, XIV). Mixed with them grow birch, pine, black spruce, tamarack – all useful for newsprint, furniture, or plywood.

To travel by canoe through such country is to leave the modern world for something so different that com-parisons do not exist. The engine is muscle, the shelter canvas, the food dehydrated or fresh killed, and the scenery beyond criticism. Even at its most dangerous or difficult, this shining country is beautiful; the rocks in the rapids shine red and gold in the spray; the uphill portage trail smells sweetly of balsam; the cry of the loon before rain is so poignant it seems almost holy. Lonely it is, but not unfriendly if you know how to use it, and certainly the people, no matter how remote they are geographically, warm you like a winter fire.

This rim of Lake Superior has only recently been opened to automobiles, with the completion of the Trans-Canada Highway. The highest point in a flat province (2,120 feet, at Tip Top Hill) stands behind these hills (plate 99) south of Superior Provincial Park.

100 MARATHON, LAKE SUPERIOR

101–103 For a Westerner coming down from Calgary to the prairies, for an Easterner coming to this WINNIPEG on the banks of the Red River, the first sight of these plains is an appalling experience. The immensity of the sky, the flatness of the land, the lack of feature and variation, are enough to make a stranger pity the people who live here, and to send him home as fast as he can go. But for the plainsman born, the shadow forms of the clouds moving immensely over the land, the sight of thunderheads a hundred miles away on the horizon bar, the feeling that your shoulders are level with eternity – these are enough to dismiss mere valleys or shores as possible homes. W. O. Mitchell has described his prairie in the opening chapter of his novel *Who Has Seen the Wind*: '. . . prairie lay wide around the town, stretching tan to the far line of the sky, shimmering under the June sun and waiting for the unfailing visitation of wind, gentle at first, barely stroking the long grasses. . . . Where the snow-white of alkali edged the course of the river, a thin trickle of water made its way toward the town low upon the horizon. Silver willow, heavy with dust, grew along the riverbanks, perfuming the air with its honey smell.'

The river and Winnipeg (plate 101) are inseparable. The Red and the Assiniboine supported the first settlements, and now, running through the city's centre, they are lined with docks and boathouses where people keep big cruisers, outboards, rowboats, and canoes, which they can use to travel miles up or down either river, and into Lake Winnipeg.

It is true that, to the traveller arriving from the east, Winnipeg, netted in poles and wires, looms on the horizon like a disaster, but there is nothing average or ugly about the life of the people here. The city has been from its foundation one of the most interesting in Canada. From the great bubble-time wittily described in Stephen Leacock's reminiscence of his Uncle Bill, when fortunes floated up and down Portage Avenue waiting for men to snatch them out of the air, through the riotous twenties and thirties, the city has always been intense and varied. It has probably more significant minorities than even Montreal: here, Scots, Icelanders Mennonites, Ukrainians, English, French, Métis (or

101 WINNIPEG, Manitoba

144

half-breeds), Jews and Christians from Russia, Poland, and Germany, and lately Americans, have come in and made a babel, usually joyful, and sometimes not.

Rivers and railways as well as races meet here. The Assiniboine joins the Red River to flow through Lake Winnipeg, then on to Hudson Bay. The C.N.R. and the C.P.R. have their great western marshalling-yards here, routeing grain down to the Lakehead at Port Arthur–Fort William. The members of the Provincial Legislature meet here (Legislative Building, plate 101, lower right). And at Winnipeg meet two extremes of weather – Arctic cold and desert heat. The January isotherm (line of mean temperature for an area), which runs by Winnipeg, stretches through the Arctic to the Pole. It is the coldest major city in Canada. The January mean is zero, and it has been as low as fifty-four below in the city. The winter temperature often stays at zero or less for four to six weeks. Yet in July the heat has been as high as a hundred and eight degrees, and temperatures of a hundred or more have been recorded in every month from May to the end of September.

When Rupert Brooke visited the city in 1913, he found that it had more promise for the future than any

102 SLOUGH, Southern Manitoba

of the other Canadian cities he had visited, because it had broken away from the prevailing mores of North America and was on its way to a destiny different from any other city's. That he was prescient has been proven amply. The Winnipeg General Strike after the war, the continuous strength of Socialism, the strength, beauty, and originality of the Royal Winnipeg Ballet, of the various dramatic groups, and of its writers (Gabrielle Roy, Jack Ludwig, Adele Wiseman) have proved that the city has a progressive drive lacking in the east, not likely to slow even under its present affluence.

Southern Manitoba, like most of the Prairies, is famous for its bird life. Sloughs, like this one (plate 102), support huge populations of duck and migrants in spring and fall. An international preservation campaign has helped to preserve the sloughs so that the birds can continue to live and breed here. The approach of spring rain to the flowered plain of southern Manitoba (plate 103) is for the farmer and hunter perhaps the most welcome sight of the year, assuring a good start to the wheat- and truck-farming of this black-earth country and a plentiful supply of water for the sloughs where the ducks breed and the migrant geese settle.

103 FIELD IN SPRING, Manitoba

104–112 Lemoine Fitzgerald, the Group of Seven painter, used to lie on his back and sketch the clouds over southern Manitoba, and Peter Varley has found the same fascination in the ranked clouds over the eastern approach to REGINA, Saskatchewan (plate 104). In the foreground is the Trans-Canada Highway, here four lanes wide, and, all round the city, farming country.

SASKATCHEWAN is a big farm, supporting 627,000 rural people, 129,000 more than live in its urban areas. In only three other provinces do the rural people now outnumber the urban. Running against the Canadian population trend, Saskatchewan declined in numbers of people between 1931 and 1941 (2.8 per cent) and 1941 and 1951 (7.2 per cent). Partly, this was because of the urban drift – farm-boys going to the cities to find jobs. But it was due as well to the dustbowl conditions that prevailed here in the droughted thirties, when, during the time of Prime Minister Bennett, farming was so unproductive that the farmers could not afford gas for their new Model T Fords and hitched them to horses – hence 'Bennett buggies'. The province has begun to grow again, but its rate is still the slowest in Canada. Unless new farming techniques open the thinly settled lakeland to the north, it is not likely to grow quickly. It is prosperous now: the 95,000 operating farmers shared $630 million net in 1963, an average of $6,750. The average for 1961, a drought year, was $1,475, and the average for the 1950s was about $3,400.

The agricultural future in Saskatchewan seems to lie in water control. The South Saskatchewan River Dam Project, now well under way, is due to irrigate half a million acres of land. By March 1961, fifty-four irrigation projects affecting a further half-million acres had been begun. There were 461 drainage and flood-control projects under way, and topographic surveys had been carried out on 200,000 acres. In a land so flat that a tussock six feet high is a geographical feature, creeks, dikes, dams, and irrigation canals mean the difference between Libyan desert and fertile grassland or farms. People throughout the West are well aware that Libya was once a fertile province of the Roman Empire.

The North Saskatchewan, which flows through a remarkably deep trench (seen here at Edmonton,

104 REGINA, Saskatchewan

looking north past the high-level auto and C.P.R. bridge towards the Provincial Government Buildings, plate 105), keeps its peace more than the Red. The river here is 140 feet wide, and the valley in which it runs is 100 feet deep, in places deeper. (Downstream to the Forks the banks average between 200 and 300 feet.) Calgary, which stands beside part of the south branch (here called the Bow) 175 miles south-west of Edmonton, is 3,540 feet above sea-level and thus 2,830 feet above the mouth of the Saskatchewan itself, where it empties into Lake Winnipeg. This drop is spread over a meandering run of about 800 miles. Where the rivers are trenched deep and irrigation does not reach, the prairies are desert-dry as in southern Alberta – cactus country (plate 112). This common cactus (*Opuntia polyacantha*) is widespread in certain parts of southern British Columbia and Alberta, parts commonly known as dry-belt, where the average annual rainfall is less than ten inches. This total seems more than it is: much of it falls in summer and is immediately drawn off the land by dry winds and hot sunshine. The low rainfall extends far into South-central Saskatchewan (around Moose Jaw, plate 106).

105 EDMONTON, Alberta

106 SOUTHERN PRAIRIE, NEAR MOOSE JAW, Saskatchewan

107 BADLANDS,
DINOSAUR VALLEY,
Alberta

Disastrous to farmers, the effects of erosion are picturesque in the Badlands (plate 107) around Drumheller in the Red Deer valley, seventy-five miles west of Calgary. Here, in dry, white-grey soil, dinosaur bones and tropical fossils are constantly being found. For a while Drumheller district did a remarkable export business in dinosaur bones: museums in eastern Canada, the United States, and Europe collected fairly complete skeletons, by now numbering over thirty.

Mr. Varley has created (plate 107) an effect reminiscent of the huge Early Egyptian temples and statues carved into rock on the Nile near Aswan, but the scale here is miniature: the area shown in the photograph measures about six feet high by nine feet wide.

The prairies have accommodated, besides 'Bennett buggies', all kinds of odd transport, including railways that run straight as a ruled line for scores of miles (plates 108, 109). The Indians first went on foot; then after the wild Spanish horses drifted north, they tamed the colts and invented the travois, a V of springy poles dragged behind the ponies, to carry children or goods. White men came upriver in *canots du nord*, light birch canoes, then in steamboats, once common and essential on the Saskatchewan. They accomplished the opening of the West in the high-wheeled, squealing Red River carts that went west from Fort Garry, shrieking like guineahens. The latest attack on distance is the pipeline: it exports both gas and oil from Alberta to eastern Canada, and technicians in Edmonton have experimented with a new type that will move solids suspended in a moving mass of fluid.

The mountain alder (plates 110, 111) is in North America a typically Western tree, growing in Canada from the mouth of the Mackenzie south to the border, and west from central Saskatchewan to the Pacific. It usually grows alone in unmixed stands that have a crinkled appearance, because the trunks are both light barked and crooked. The leaves (plate 110) are coarse and hairy.

154

110 ALDER LEAF, Alberta

112 DESERT CACTUS, Southern Alberta

111 ALDER BLUFF, WILLOW VALLEY, Alberta

113 CALGARY, Alberta

113–122, XVI The eastern foothills of the Rocky Mountains are among the loveliest regions of Canada. The prairie, which rises almost imperceptibly in shallow steps towards CALGARY (plate 113), here breaks up into tremendous ranges, not quite mountains but hinting at the sea of mountains beyond, no longer prairie but fertile as the blackest of Manitoba land. In the south, the main streams, many flowing from the Columbia Glacier high in the Rockies, are tributaries of the Mississippi or the Saskatchewan. In the Peace River country to the north, the land is watered by the Peace, flowing from its sources in the Rocky Mountain Trench to the Arctic. Among these hills, the towns, such as High River, begin to feel the effects of the Pacific on trade (plate 115) and on climate. Although Calgary is 3,500 feet above sea-level, it is much warmer through winter than lower prairie cities, because the hot chinook winds keep the atmosphere dry, clear, and warm. The chinooks originate in the Pacific, when wet air rises slowly up the west flank of the mountains, cooling as it expands at the higher altitudes, and losing its moisture. When it flows down the east side of the mountains, it warms up again by compression at the lower altitudes. The warming rate of the dried air is roughly twice the cooling rate of the ascending wet air. The chinook effect is most dramatic on a cold January day: there is a hesitant feeling in the atmosphere – suddenly the bright western air, a sharp line against the polar clouds, shoves the clouds to the east, the temperature leaps up as much as sixty degrees in a couple of hours, and the snow on the ground vanishes without a trace. The chinook helps to keep the average Calgary January mean at a tolerable fifteen degrees, while Winnipeg (zero) and Edmonton (seven degrees) suffer.

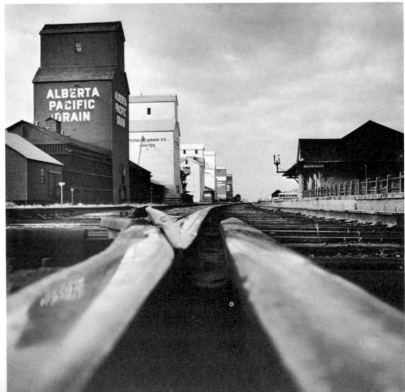

The sense of space, of plentiful land and air for every human being, which Indian tribes east and west seem to have shared, still exists among the Indians of the Stony Reserve in the foothills of Alberta (plate 114). Though of different linguistic background, the Stony Reserve Indians, like the Cree-Iroquoian of Christian Island, Georgian Bay, have set their houses much farther apart than white men would. The southern part of the reserve, south of the Bow River, has recently been opened by the Trans-Canada Highway section running to Banff.

The saddle horses (also called ponies, Indian ponies, and pintos, plates 116, 119) of the West are still used for rounding up cattle, or for riding for pleasure through the foothills country. A man may saddle up at his own barn at dawn, with his son, carrying fishing-rods, and ride to a trout pool on a river such as the Highwood (here seen twenty-five miles west of High River, Alberta, plates 117, XVI), and pull out half a dozen brook trout for breakfast; here, the Highwood is still a clear mountain stream. He will spend the rest of the day in a valley such as this one (plate 118) south of the Highwood and east of Mount Burke, 8,360 feet, where

his cattle have excellent grassland. His business is done in a little town such as Pincher Creek (population 2,961), only a few miles from the first abrupt surge of the mountains (plate 120, looking south towards Victoria Peak, 8,460 feet, and Mount Haig, 8,565). Willow Valley (plate 122) is in the southern foothills, shaded from the west by the eastern ridge of the Rockies, which separate it from the Kananaskis River valley on the far side.

From Cowley, Alberta, near the United States border, Highway 3 runs towards Crow's Nest Pass in the southern Rockies. Here the mountains rise very steeply from relatively level plateau land. Crow's Nest Mountain is 9,138 feet high, and the prevailing heights are

120 PINCHER CREEK, Alberta

8,000 to 9,000 feet. Near here the famous Frank Slide occurred in 1903: after a short earth-tremor, about ninety million tons of rock fell from Turtle Mountain on the town of Frank in the Crow's Nest Pass. Sixty-six people died under the rock. Although the slide was later estimated to have lasted only two minutes, perhaps less, it covered a square mile of the valley to a depth of forty-five feet. Marks of smaller slides are visible in many of the mountain illustrations (including plate 122, centre and left).

The fences along Highway 3 (plate 121) are permanent snow fences. Annual snowfall in this area is about eighty inches, drifted over the highways by the prevailing south-west wind.

122 WILLOW VALLEY, Alberta ▶

121 APPROACHING CROW'S NEST
PASS, Alberta

123–127   Yellowknife (plate 123), NORTHWEST
TERRITORIES, on the north shore of Great Slave Lake
(sixty-two degrees N.) is at roughly the same latitude
as Bergen, Norway, where rhododendrons grow wild,
but the Canadian town is in the forest and barren
region of Canada, sub-arctic in climate, and only 200 or
so miles from the tree-line (beyond which trees cannot
grow). The January mean daily temperature, fourteen
below zero, is bitter, but humidity is relatively low and
the winds are light. The growing season is long for the
Canadian inland region – both July and August are
frost-free in the average year, and there is usually only
one night in June with frost. (Whitehorse, nearer the
Pacific, farther south, and generally warmer, nevertheless has more summer frost because it is higher – 2,289
feet to Yellowknife's 682.)

First settled in 1934 during a gold rush, Yellowknife
was largely deserted until 1944, when the rush resumed.
The population now is 3,200, up from 2,700 in 1951,
and the town is an important way-point on routes to
the Far North.

Two places on the Coppermine River, 400 air-miles
to the north, have been served by Yellowknife. Sixty
miles from the river-mouth town and well beyond the
tree-line, Canadian scientists at Speers Lake worked on
the Upper Mantle Project in 1963, probing with hard-
rock drilling equipment (flown up from North Bay,
Ontario, via Yellowknife) a mile into the earth's upper
mantle (the layer immediately below the earth's crust)
to discover its composition and characteristics. A pre-
liminary discovery was that the permafrost, or permanently frozen layer of surface earth, was about 700 feet
deep in this area.

On the Coppermine River, just south of the Dismal
Lakes, the upper mantle appears in a fault at the surface
of the earth – a rare occurrence. Fuel for running the
drills (plates 124, 127), flown up in steel drums, is stored
outdoors. After use, the drums, worth nine dollars each,
are abandoned, because to fly them back would be too
expensive.

Isachsen (plates 125, 126) on Ellef Ringnes Island
(seventy-nine degrees N.) is one of the Far North's
remotest settlements. Primarily a weather station,

123 YELLOWKNIFE, Northwest
Territories

124 COPPERMINE RIVER, Northwest Territories

operated jointly by Canada and the United States,
Isachsen began as an exploration base for the federal
government's Polar Continental Shelf Project, accom-
modating up to seventy or eighty scientists and technicians doing a dozen different kinds of survey and
research work in the Arctic islands. Primitive and modern
methods combine oddly: the helicopter (plate 125) flew
out over the ocean and landed on the ice, where the
scientists chopped a hole in the ice and lowered a hand-
line to find the depth and get a sample of the ocean floor.

170

125 ISACHSEN, ELLEF RINGNES ISLAND, 79° N., Northwest Territories

126 ISACHSEN

127 COPPERMINE RIVER, MACKENZIE DISTRICT, Northwest Territories

XIII LAKE HURON, NEAR SOUTHAMPTON, Ontario

XIV NORTH SHORE, LAKE SUPERIOR

XIII The Indians called this lake 'The Shining Sea' and told Champlain, when he first came onto it in summer, that the sun set in it every night and that they had never seen its farther shore. Champlain, reaching Georgian Bay at French River, wondered if this immensity were part of the Pacific, and reached over the side of the canoe to taste the water. To him it became the Sweet Sea.

Up this coast of LAKE HURON near Southampton sailed first the ship of the white men, La Salle's *Griffon*, wrecked possibly at the north end of the coast, near Tobermory. Then, after the battle of Put-in-Bay in 1813, three ships of the United States Navy sailed past here to blockade the British and Canadians at Manitoulin Island. They were later captured by a small British-Canadian force, and the lake, with most of the North American West, remained British Canada's till the end of the War of 1812. Through a century and a half of peace, first wooden sailing ships, then small black iron steamers, followed by huge red freighters, with the typical lake ship's long, low line, have sailed by here loaded with the goods of the prosperous regions that spread all round the southern Great Lakes.

The boy with his outboard returning home at sunset is a familiar scene in these great waters.

XIV The northern shores of LAKE SUPERIOR are still wild enough that people can travel for hundreds of miles camping every night through summer, most of the time far from civilization.

172

128–130 The YUKON is boom-and-bust country – first the gold rush of the 1890s, then the wartime defence boom, then the great festival of 1962 in Dawson. Unique in the North, the festival attracted stars from Broadway (Bert Lahr) and from Toronto (Pierre Berton). Crowds of tourists gave Dawson some of its old glamour and beat. Inspired by the same Tom Patterson who revivified Stratford, Ontario, the Dawson Festival was supposed to attract hordes of tourists up the Alaska Highway. The festival was sponsored by the federal, territorial, and municipal governments, and thus got off to a good financial start. However, the 20,000 tourists who came did not spend enough, and the deficit of $396,000 became a comic point in debates in the House of Commons.

129 BLACK MIKE WINAGE

128 MOOSEHIDE, DAWSON CITY, Yukon

There were moments during the festival when it seemed Dawson might be on the rebound, moments like those when Black Mike Winage (plate 129), dressed up for the occasion, leaned out of the royal box at the Palace Grand Theatre and started to shout jokes at Bert Lahr during the world première of the musical *Foxy* by Ring Lardner, Jr., and Ian M. Hunter. Black Mike, born in Serbia, lived in Dawson after 1898, when he came up to mine gold.

175

Viewed from a side-hill near Suicide Point, on the trail to the Indian village of Moosehide, some of Black Mike's Dawson streets run along the river-front just above the point where the Klondike River (left) enters the Yukon (plate 130). During gold-rush days the home of about 25,000 people, Dawson has a population of about 850 today.

A couple of miles upriver from Dawson is the Indian settlement of Moosehide, where the Horst Sheffer family lives (plate 128). Descendants of a German settler who married a Loucheux Indian woman, the Scheffers live in a log cabin (thirty feet by fifteen feet) faced near the entrance with boards. The typical occupations of the settlement are trapping in winter and fishing or hunting in summer. Close to the river, the settlement is connected to Dawson only by a rough trail in off-season or by the river in winter and summer. There are no streets at Moosehide, only trails from one house to another, with wide spaces separating the houses. A school building stands on the settlement's grounds, but there is no teacher. A portrait of Queen Elizabeth on the schoolhouse wall has been shot by a rifle bullet and some of the windows are broken.

130 DAWSON CITY, Yukon

176

131 KANANASKIS RIVER, Alberta

THE ROCKIES AND THE SELKIRKS

131–136 Last in the tremendous geographical experiences of Canadians – the Great River, the Great Lakes, the Great Plains, the ROCKIES – these mountains have been pierced but not civilized. Edward Blake, the Liberal leader opposing the Confederation railway schemes of the 1870s, told the House of Commons at Ottawa that at that time it was madness to try to build a railway 'through that sea of mountains'. The nation disagreed, and in July 1886 Prime Minister John A. Macdonald with his wife, Susan Agnes, was riding the cow-catcher of a C.P.R. locomotive as it headed west, sometimes straight through the mountains – the Connaught Tunnel in the Selkirk Range is five miles long.

178

132 PEYTO LAKE, Alberta

Rolling hills almost a mile high, subtropical Yucca grass, rivers that run to the Caribbean, scorpions, sagebrush, cactus – Saskatchewan. Here in the Cypress Hills (plate xv) in the south-west corner of the province a beautiful hill country of a thousand square miles belies the typical conception of Saskatchewan, of Canada itself. Edward McCourt's fine description of antelope in this country is a reminder of wild days not yet over:

XV CYPRESS HILLS, Saskatchewan

'Fine herds of antelope – a glorious sight on the skyline of a far-off ridge or hill – roam . . . all the way from the border north into the country of the Great Sandhills. In the hunting season . . . it is possible to stand on a high point at the edge of the Cypress Hills Provincial Park and see herds of antelope streaming across the plains towards the Park. . . .' (From *Saskatchewan* by Edward McCourt.)

The triviality of what men do is nowhere in Canada so apparent as here: not only may the railways or highways be destroyed in a moment by millions of tons of rock washing them away like water melting sand, but, even where the mountains do not threaten physically, they amuse by the scale they set against our cabins and bridges. A trapper's cabin seven feet high is built alone on a mountain standing 12,000 feet high; on a valley fence encircling a peak a sign reads 'Private Property' and you look up to the peak, its tip in private clouds.

If in North America these mountains are big, they are tremendous by European standards: in height the

133 GLACIER NATIONAL PARK, British Columbia

134 C.P.R. BRIDGE, MOUNT TUPPER

135 HERMIT RANGE, SELKIRK MOUNTAINS, British Columbia

Alps range down from Mount Blanc (15,782 feet), and they extend to the east a few hundred miles and are only a few score miles across. The North American Cordillera runs for thousands of miles from north to south; the Rocky chain alone reaches a width of a hundred miles, and is only one of three main chains which together are 600 miles wide in many places, from foothills to mountainous sea-coast. The highest of the Canadian mountains, Mount Logan, in the St. Elias Range, Yukon, is 4,000 feet higher than Mont Blanc. Norwegians who have ridden the famous Bergen-Oslo railway come back from the C.P.R. or the C.N.R. lines in British

XVI HIGHWOOD RIVER, Alberta

Columbia saying that their own line is small stuff compared with the Canadian ones; but, more surprisingly, they come back in awe from their visits to the fiords of British Columbia, stunned to realize that their own fiords are so small, so short, by comparison.

After the great railway-building, when the mountains were first pierced by permanent forms of transportation (the fur-traders were the first to cross by foot and canoe, ahead of even the Indians), there was a lag in the attack on the valleys. A few roads were built; Trans-Canada Air Lines opened its first trans-mountain passenger service in March 1938 with Lockheed 10 aircraft. Now, the Trans-Canada Highway crosses the Rocky Range between Lake Louise and the Golden-Donald Station road, where it turns west, following much the same country as the C.P.R. line, but opening for the first time to automobile traffic the spectacular country from Rogers Pass (named after Major A. B. Rogers who explored it for the C.P.R. in 1881) down to Glacier. This straight-line cut-off saves motorists the 170-mile loop trip over a poor road from Donald to Revelstoke. The country through which tourists may now drive on a modern, long-curved, shallow-grade highway is typified by the photographs of the Rockies (in the Kananaskis River country, plate 131; at Peyto Lake, twenty-six miles north of Banff, plate 132), and of the Selkirks (plate 136). After he crosses the Rockies, the tourist runs fourteen miles up the Rocky Mountain Trench from Golden to Donald Station, then turns in towards Rogers Pass: Before the construction scars healed, he could look straight into the darkness of the full evergreen forest, without the impediment of underbrush (plate 133). On the eastern slope of Mount Tupper (9,239 feet), near Glacier, he will see this C.P.R. bridge (plate 134) joining two mountains, and all around will be mountains such as these (plates 135, 136) in the Hermit Range, which averages 8,000 to 10,000 feet above sea-level. The Western white spruce (plate 135, left) is common in this area, with lodgepole pine, Engelmann spruce, Rocky Mountain fir, and Douglas fir. In this latitude, the spruce grow at altitudes of 3,000 to 6,000 feet, neatly marking off for the practised eye the heights of all the mountains in sight.

186

136 HERMIT RANGE, SELKIRK MOUNTAINS, British Columbia

137–138, XVII In the spring of 1807, while the snow was deep on the Rocky Mountains, David Thompson left the North Saskatchewan River with ten pack-horses and headed west. He came to a place where 'mountain connected to mountain by immense glaciers, the collection of ages'. He crossed to a fast stream flowing north, later named the Columbia, and then turned south. Beside a long lake amid mountains he built Kootenae House, the first trading-post on the Columbia River basin. In this marvellous long valley today are grassland (plates 137, XVII), mines, farms, towns, and fading mementoes of the earliest days (plate 138, the church at FORT STEELE).

Thompson looked for furs, among other things, and the ensuing trade of the North West Company in the area bore out his faith in building Kootenae House.

After the Nor' Wester era came government, with the establishment of a North West Mounted Police post at Fort Steele in 1887. This was the first N.W.M.P. fort in British Columbia. The church attached to the fort still stands, though disused (plate 138).

The steep nature of the Rocky Mountain Trench, down whose east flank Thompson descended, is clear here in the shot taken across grassland looking towards Fernie (plate 137). The mountains here range from 7,000 to 9,000 feet, and Crow's Nest Pass, through them, is 4,500 feet.

138 CHURCH, FORT STEELE

137 RANGE LAND, CRANBROOK, British Columbia

Where the clouds touch the grass, at altitudes between 1,500 and 3,500 feet along the southern slopes of these hills, grows the Ponderosa pine (plates 137, XVII). Common in the western United States, the Ponderosa – orange-barked, deeply cleft when old, and tall (160– 180 feet) – grows from the southern Rockies west almost to the Fraser at about Lillooet, but not on the coast. The broken twigs have a light, sharp smell like crushed orange-peel. (Thompson's description, from his narrative, is quoted in *British Columbia: a History*, by Margaret A. Ormsby.)

191

139–142, XVIII 'This whole area is lifted into a lighter, paler feeling than I have ever experienced before,' wrote Peter Varley after photographing the country round the KOOTENAY LAKES. 'All the colour tones are lighter, the water is pale green (plate XVIII), even the evergreens seem lighter. The textures of things here are rough

XVIII KOOTENAY LAKE, British Columbia

192

(except for the wave-washed pebbles, plate 142): the rocks, the Ponderosa pine-bark – even the weather. This lake has amazingly quick storms.' Part of the reason for this is the character of the lake and the shore. Although Kootenay Lake is over sixty miles long, its area is only 168 square miles, and the mountains at each side rise abruptly to 7,000 to 8,000 feet, which is 5,500 to 6,500 feet above the lake level (see plate 139, the steep shore at the narrows near Balfour).

In the past, the mountain walls echoed with the sound of steam-whistles as paddle-wheelers took supplies in from the north end of the Arrow Lakes–Kootenay system; now the boats are modern ferries, carrying cars (plate 139, near Nelson) and sport-fishing boats (plate 141), built for rod-fishing such game fish as Kamloops cut-throat, Kokanee and Dolly Varden trout, and large-mouthed bass. Fishing here and in the Okanagan lasts from April to November. Kootenay and Okanagan lakes rarely freeze over.

Wrinkled and twisted like driftwood, the mountainous west shore of the lake (seen from Boswell on the east side, three miles across, plate 140) rises steeply to Ymir Mountain (7,920 feet), seven miles inland. The C.P.R.'s Kettle Valley–Crow's Nest line runs along the west lakeshore.

139 NELSON FERRY, KOOTENAY LAKE

140, 141, 142 KOOTENAY LAKE, British Columbia

143-144 The misapprehension of Canada as a cold country is exposed in the DRY-BELT REGION of southern British Columbia (as well as on the coast and in southern Ontario), not just by dry belt cactus and sagebrush, but by cash crops of such fruits as the Moorpark, Tilton, and Blenheim apricots, which are so tender that they scarcely ripen in England unless carefully protected and trained against a sheltering wall. But here, apricot orchards produce scores of thousands of bushels a year: the total production in Canada varies from a quarter to a third of a million bushels a year, grown here and in southern Ontario.

The dry belt, whose south-eastern corner is at Grand Forks (plate 143), extends to the north-west as far as the Thompson River near its exit from Kamloops Lake (plate 144). Throughout most of this large area, measuring roughly 10,000 square miles, the annual precipitation is ten inches or less, and the farms, especially the orchards, depend on irrigation. All the major irrigation projects in British Columbia in 1962 were in this area (except for a few in the adjacent Columbia and Kettle River valleys, which lie in the same rain shadow, extending east from the coast range).

About 35,000 acres were irrigated under these projects, with a further 18,000 potentially irrigable. Total of lands previously irrigated in British Columbia is 218,000, again chiefly in the dry belt. The water comes from the clear, cold mountain streams which in most cases come parallel straight down the slopes to the valley rivers, like ribs on a fishbone.

The Thompson (plate 144, near Savona) is clear and fresh, with benchlands and low side-hills covered with shimmering grasses and sagebrush. The low light in the photograph brings out the peculiar sheen of these grasses.

143 DRY-BELT FARM, GRAND FORKS, British Columbia

144 THOMPSON RIVER IN THE DRY BELT

145–146 The excitement that grips you coming into the Upper Fraser Valley is extraordinary: everyone with a feel for land senses it. The river is huge and young and wild: in spring flood, as much water rushes through the 160-foot gap at Hell's Gate as normally flows in the mile-wide St. Lawrence at Quebec. The upper river is a wild mountain stream, pitching down staircases of rock, tearing at its banks (plate 146, lower left), so swollen in spring that it appears to bulge up in the middle (plate 145). The violence of the water's rush appears impressively at the junction with the Thompson. In Hugh MacLennan's words: 'The Thompson is the Fraser's chief tributary, a major stream in its own right, and it does not so much enter the Fraser as smash its way into it like a liquid battering ram. From the bridge (at Lytton) I saw its water plunging into the Fraser . . . blue-green into the yellow froth. Then it completely disappeared. The Fraser swallows the Thompson in less than a hundred yards.' (From *Seven Rivers of Canada*.)

So loud in many places that people on shore cannot hear each other talk, the Fraser runs down its 400-mile canyon to Hope, where it widens and slows and begins to meander through a broad valley towards the sea at Vancouver. Seen near Hell's Gate thirty miles above Hope, the canyon carries on the west side (plate 145, right) the main C.P.R. transcontinental line and on the east the Cariboo Highway and the C.N.R. line.

Viewed to the north from the place where the road between Lillooet and Pavilion leaves the Fraser Valley (plate 146), the Fraser turns between high hillsides running up at an angle of about forty-five degrees. In the distance is the Camelsfoot Range (5,000–7,000 feet). The land is as dry as it looks, and skies as clear as these prevail in the area, which lies in the rain shadow of the Coast Range. Ashcroft, near by, gets 7.4 inches of precipitation in an average year.

198

145 FRASER CANYON, British Columbia

146 FRASER RIVER NEAR LILLOOET

147 FARM NEAR KITWANGA, British Columbia

148 MT. CATT, SKEENA VALLEY

149 SKEENA RIVER

147–149 The mountains round the SKEENA RIVER are, for height visible to the eye, among the most impressive in the country, for they rise sharply from about sea-level to 6,000 feet within a mile or so of the river (plate 149, near Terrace) and achieve 9,000 feet ten or fifteen miles inland from there. The Seven Sisters Range (plate 147) is 9,140 feet high just six miles south from Woodcock on the river.

The river itself is navigable for coastal craft, a hundred miles from its mouth near Prince Rupert, just south of the tip of the Alaska Panhandle.

The salmon fishing in this river, round the estuary, especially from mid-July to the end of September, is dazzling. In 1959, the world record for spring salmon was set in the estuary of the Skeena with the landing of a ninety-two-pound tyee on a rod. This tidal slough (plate 148), near Kwinitsa, is just upriver from the estuary. The smaller coho salmon are abundant here too, and may, unlike other salmon, be fished right up the river into the spawning streams. One of those streams runs in the wooded valley just behind the frame farm-house (plate 147) in the valley north of the Seven Sisters Mountains. The farmer can hunt for mule deer or Columbia blacktail (60,000 deer are taken in an average year in the province) or for the many upland game birds, including various grouse and ptarmigan.

201

150 BURIAL HOUSE, KITWANCOOL, British Columbia

151 TOTEMS, KITWANCOOL

152 BURIAL HOUSE, KITWANCOOL

150–152 This Tsimshian Indian graveyard near Hazelton is typical of many with its mixture of poles (plates 150, 151) and burial-houses (plate 152). Occasionally, the houses, or carved coffins, were suspended on the arms of one of the poles.

The poles were originally carved with stone tools from cedar trunks, and used as decoration for houses or sometimes as actual supports, usually at the front, holding up floor joists. With the arrival of white men, metal tools became available and pole-carving grew more popular, reaching its peak in the 1890s, after which it began to decline. Paint was used to decorate the features, but the artistic essence of the family pole was stylized sculpture. Among the rank-conscious Tsimshian, the poles, some of them ninety feet high, also came to represent wealth and influence. New poles were dedicated at a potlatch, a marvellous ceremony in which the host achieved everlasting fame by giving away enormous quantities of blankets, slaves, furs, food, and canoes. There was an element of competition – a rival might try to achieve greatest credit by giving away more, and a touch of canny investment – the rival might outdo the host by returning the gifts with interest. This ceremony, one of the important parts of West Coast Indian life, has been banned by the Canadian government, with the result that former Indian shrines such as these have fallen into ruin.

153–157 Of these poles, Peter Varley wrote: '. . . a Tsimshian pole leans, rotting at the base. Its carving is strange and spiritual, reminiscent of Mayan culture far to the south, seemingly abstracting the qualities of its environment but having even deeper roots. The flaming suns carved by the Tsimshian are oval in outline, and are oddly negative in feeling. The pole is a symbol of creation perceived by a sensitive people tuned to their spiritual life, to the earth, and to the whole mysterious universe.'

Mungo Martin, one of the last of the Coast carvers, created this expressive pole (plate 153) in the late 1940s. It shows, from top to bottom, a raven, a killer whale, and an Indian chief. This, with the pole in plate 157, is in the Totem Park at the University of British Columbia in Vancouver. The pole in plate 157 was carved before 1939 on the north part of the British Columbia coast; information about it is scanty because no testimony from the family that commissioned it exists now. This situation extends over much of Canadian Indian life, combated only by a few researchers, often private, occasionally with foundation or government grants. Totem Park has been extended to include a Haida village with poles, dwelling-house, and grave-house.

Typical of the environment in which these Indians lived are these plants and mosses (plates 154–6). The trailing moss (*Hypnum circinale*), and the leafy moss (*Mnium glabrescens*), both growing on the log (plate 154), are found only in humid forests of the West Coast of North America.

The moss encircling the cedar log (plate 155) is *Plagiothecium undulatum*, a West Coast moss that grows only in damp coniferous forests.

The Indian pipe (plate 156) grows on decayed vegetable matter – old stumps and rotten fallen logs – in conifer forests.

157 TOTEM, VANCOUVER

158–164 VANCOUVER is a beautiful city. The mountains, the forests, and the Gulf of Georgia surround it with a natural beauty that is visible from any part of the city. Many of the residential streets are exceptionally wide, edged with gardens that bloom ten or eleven months of the year; the residential architecture is the most advanced of any large city in Canada; the sea air blows in pure and sweet from the gulf; and even the pestilential fogs that settle in for days at a time in winter have a lovely aspect viewed from the height of Lions Gate Bridge.

It began as a lumber town in the 1860s, centred on a tavern kept by Gassy Jack Deighton. Lumber is still vital to Vancouver, but the old forests that stood here at the mouth of the Fraser River are gone, except for the remnant in Stanley Park. The logs (chiefly spruce and fir, plate 158) come down the coast in Davis rafts towed by tugboats to Vancouver's mills for processing into plywood, pulp, and lumber. Hollyburn Ridge (plate 158, background) rises above the downtown skyline, seen from False Creek in the centre of town. The British Columbia Power Commission Building, one among many new modern commercial buildings in the city, stands at right, behind the C.P.R. yards.

The city is too new to have a defined character yet, but there are signs of the way it must develop. The early tendency to variety, when the town was wide open to all kinds of people, shut off abruptly with the passing of discriminatory immigration laws. The laws were disallowed by Ottawa; nevertheless they reduced the influx of East Indians, Japanese, and Chinese (plate 159, the old Chinatown on West Pender Street). Today, immigrants from Europe and eastern Canada, and a few from Asia, are slowly threading new colours into the Anglo-Saxon cloth. From a close concentration on money and politics, Vancouver has turned to a wary interest in 'useless' things. Its painters – Bobak, Smith, Binning – were among the best in Canada during a post-war surge of creative activity here, and its writers – Earle Birney, George Bowering, Eric Nicol, and the sad visitor, Malcolm Lowry – produced some of the

207

158 VANCOUVER FROM FALSE CREEK, British Columbia

160 QUEEN ELIZABETH PARK,
VANCOUVER

161 RESIDENCE, HOWE SOUND

most interesting writing in Canada in the fifties and
sixties. Vancouver buildings have won national prizes
(e.g. the Massey Gold Medal for architecture for Thea
Koerner House at the University of British Columbia),
and the new Massey College in Toronto was designed
by a member of a Vancouver firm. The post-and-beam
house, whose first thorough development in Canada
was here, is prevalent in the suburbs (plate 161, overlooking Howe Sound, north of Vancouver). The post-
and-beam house has been widely imitated in the rest of
Canada. Sports – racing, football, swimming, rowing,
golf, tennis – are all phenomenally popular, largely
owing to the long season. The University of British
Columbia, which is both big and very progessive in its
attitudes, has outlived the time when Easterners condes-
cended to its awkwardness, and is now recognized as
one of the best universities in Canada.

When you look down to the end of a street in
Vancouver, often you are staring into a green sea of

208

leaves. This is not always a case of haphazard development into the surrounding rain forest, for Vancouver people have freckled their city with parks. The biggest, Stanley Park, has formidable crowds, trees, and zoo; the smaller ones, like Queen Elizabeth Park (plate 160), are simply refreshing. Queen Elizabeth Park is laid out in a pleasant rambling pattern on various levels and the paths connecting the gardens are left relatively wild.

In most parts of the city, there is a remarkable sense of not being in a city at all. When you stand on Georgia Street, downtown, and can look up at Hollyburn, or Grouse Mountain (3,900 feet); when you drive home from work over Lions Gate Bridge to North or West Vancouver and look west over deep sea, the sense of release from pressure is blessed. Often on a warm day, office-workers take a sandwich lunch down to the shore at English Bay, an arc of sand built up by the Fraser. The river's yellow sands boil out into the gulf and are pushed back to shore by tide and wind, where they have built up English Bay and a whole peninsula of beaches round Point Grey. At Spanish Banks (plate 162) on this shore, great logs broken away from the log booms are washed up. People frequently come down to cut off a piece and chop it up for firewood. They run the risk of being caught by logging company officials, for the stamp driven into the end of the softwood logs compacts the fibres into the owner's brand ten feet or more down the length of the log.

The clouds that hang over Vancouver are familiar (plate 164, looking at the city from Lions Gate Bridge, Stanley Park, in front of the downtown area). The city is the dullest in Canada during the winter months, as well as the rainiest. The view reversed (plate 163) shows the Lions Gate Bridge from Vancouver Harbour.

162 SPANISH BANKS, VANCOUVER

163, 164 VANCOUVER HARBOUR

165–167 Burrard Inlet, a long, narrow street of water lined on both sides with docks, begins just east of here (plate 167), between Point Atkinson (foreground) and Point Grey (upper left). The inlet is Vancouver's harbour, the dividing line between residential North Vancouver and downtown, and the obstacle between the city proper and the mainland to the north. Vancouver is Canada's second port in terms of total tonnage loaded and unloaded each year. Only Montreal handles more goods. By far the most important of the goods trans-shipped here is wheat, almost double the tonnage of the next bulkiest item, pulpwood and chips. The wheat comes down from the prairies by rail, and goes out from here to the world, including Red China and Russia.

The Gulf of Georgia (to the right) lies between the mainland and Vancouver Island, which is just visible through the mist (at upper centre and upper right). Over this gulf comes Vancouver's wet winter weather: the clouds gathered over the gulf, and the Pacific beyond, drive inland, blown by the prevailing westerlies. Lying on the edge of the Pacific, Victoria on Vancouver Island has a noticeably warmer, drier, and brighter winter, because of the influence of the relatively warm sea, which protects the whole southern tip of the island from cold polar air, and because its surrounding land is low. The warm, damp air from the Pacific can pass over Victoria at a low altitude, but it must rise to pass over the coast wall backing Vancouver; and there, cooled, it turns to fog or rain. Vancouver does not get a remarkable number of inches of rain (only fifty-four in the average year, plus two feet of snow), but what it does get is concentrated in winter and spread over a disheartening number of days (average: twenty-five in December, twenty-three in January, including snowy days). Still, there is a place on the island, called Henderson Lake, which makes this seem arid: at Henderson Lake were set several North American rain records – 323 inches in a year, and eighty inches in one month. The south end of Vancouver Island (twenty-five inches in an average year) is indisputably the pleasantest place in Canada to live. The gardening season is virtually year-round; there have been winters with no frost at

212

165 STRAITS OF JUAN DE FUCA, British Columbia

166 VANCOUVER ISLAND

all; in most, there are fewer than twenty nights of it, even fewer days.

At Point No Point, near Victoria, on the Straits of Juan de Fuca, between the southern end of the island and the American mainland, the polished black rocks smoothed by tide and wave rise like whalebacks (plate 165). The tides here are relatively low and the earth is covered with shore grasses (plate 166) almost to the edge of the water, even at low tide. You seldom see that long extent of tidal foreshore, wet, puddled, and stinking of the sea, so common in the east. Along the coast here, if there is such a low shore, it is often covered at low tide with abalone-pickers wading out in hipboots to take the molluscs from the rocks.

These straits between the small Canadian off-shore islands and the American ones in the distance (plate 165, background, includes the Canadian islands nearest camera, with the Olympic Mountains of the United States in the far background) are the last of Canada for ships heading west. The ocean is in a lull here, but when the gales come, as they frequently do in winter, the coast disappears under the flying spray of waves fifty feet high. The worst storms are from the south-east (camera direction, due south). At such moments these summer-blown drift logs, probably broken loose from a raft far to the north, are picked up and thrown scores of feet inland.

In summer, the season when these photographs were taken, the shore is delightful. The swimming season is short (from June to early September) considering the mild winters. The reason is that it takes the ocean months to warm up. The air temperature, directly influenced by the ocean, rises at a rate which for Canada is remarkably slow in spring – less than ten degrees difference in the means of March and May. The change in fall is similar – less than twelve degrees difference between September and November. Given a warm day, you come after your swim at Point No Point up the hill to an English-style teahouse overlooking the ocean, where you can have wine with your dinner of fresh Coast salmon. Canada has come no closer to serenity than this.

167 GULF OF GEORGIA, British Columbia

Index of Localities

Italic figures refer to illustrations